DRACONIA

UNICURSAL

Copyright © 2003 Marc-André Ricard
maricard.com

Éditions Unicursal Publishers
unicursal.ca

(Paperback) ISBN 978-2-89806-295-7
(Hardcover) ISBN 978-2-89806-296-4

First English Edition, Ostara 2022

M~A RICARD

DRACONIA

Draconic Teachings
of True Dragon Magick

DRACONIA BOOK 1

UNICURSAL

With my humblest thanks to Master Arion and to PNFYR, my noble guide and faithful winged companion for his help, kindness and inspiration.

And a deep thought for ZETA, my old friend, who patiently stood by my side until the very end...

INTRODUCTION

THIS book is not the product or the work of a creative mind. It tells things as they are, and only the truth. It is nothing more than a "Dragon Bible".

Knowledge and wisdom have always existed. Human beings have never, so to speak, truly invented what is, or will be in the future. For the inspired man is able to connect himself, to tap into the source of information, directly to the reservoir of knowledge, to then, put this wisdom on paper and share it with all those who wish to perfect their learning and reach perfection.

And so, this is how the teachings of Draconia were given to me and revealed through my winged and very wise counselor; PNFYR or *Pinifère* in common language.

Draconia — the Magick of Dragons — is a unique book. Never have you seen such a book and this is why it will be so valuable to you. It is an esoteric system of Ceremonial High Magick, a complete magickal training that works mainly with the help and support of dragons and the omnipresent Draconic Force. This is one of the splendors of Hermetism.

Dragons have always existed; they have been portrayed mainly in fairy tales and old legends, too often falsely exposed as being of a malevolent or evil nature. Fortunately, that is not the case at all. On the contrary, they are archetypes of power, nobility, and great wisdom.

However, despite the many opinions about dragons, an essential point of their personality remains constant. No matter what has been said about these magnificent beings, the same observation keeps surfacing: dragons are creatures buried in the depths of their lairs and jealously guard coveted treasures of great wealth.

Thus, it is true dragons are the guardians and keepers of many treasures; unlike the legends of the past, however, these fabulous riches are not made of gold coins or jewels, rubies or precious pearls. In fact, the true treasure that has always remained under the care of dragons is none other than a truly astonishing and admirable esoteric and spiritual knowledge, extremely powerful and of considerable value...

That being said, a parallel seems obvious. Remember these folk tales, all the stories about so-called "high deeds" of mighty knights going in search of glory and fighting these huge winged and malignant creatures. Protected by their shields to guard them against the powerful flames of the dragons, these men in shining armor tried the impossible to slay them and to take away their most precious possession.

These fictionalized stories projected the image that man was good and that, unfortunately, dragons were treacherous and evil. This is the error of human conception; indeed, this shows how close we were to the authentic facts and the very true nature of Draconic Beings.

What remains true to this day is that man, in his jealousy and thirst for power, has always tried to take by force what belonged to others for the sole purpose of ruling and controlling. In other words, many have tried and still are trying to fight the dragon (in various forms and symbolism), with the sole aim of obtaining control and power conferred by the knowledge of esoteric secrets. Unfortunately, the truth was misunderstood or, indeed, veiled, and the persecuted draconic creatures were given several derogatory titles such as "disloyal or dishonest beasts."

Until today, very few people could claim to practice true Draconic Magick. This Art as old as the Earth was practically forgotten by our peers, some of whom held the keys of Draconia. Only a few chosen ones were able to express the joy of working under the close companionship and spiritual knowledge of dragons.

So why is it that many of us feel more than ever this strong attraction toward these famous beings? It is my opinion that the most plausible explanation is that, since the entire Universe is made of vibrations and energies, and that all living creatures are intimately interconnected by this invisible bond, we are sensitive and, therefore, able to unconsciously feel the effects of their occult workings and their presence among us, near, almost palpable, though without realizing it.

This book has been written for all those who are interested in seriously practicing this Art and Science that is Draconic Magick, a beam of light flowing from the Central

Sun, for all those who also wish to inquire about authentic and true teachings. It is not a vulgar recipe book, simplified and meaningless, labeled under the seal of ease as are too frequently books on White Magick. Dragon Magick reveals the true paths, so you can fulfill your own destiny doing it the right way, the only there is.

Draconic Magick is not a hobby, nor a way to entertain and chase away boredom. Neither is it something that is practiced from time to time only when a situation is beyond our control. Magick is the most serious thing; it's a dedicated way of life.

Indeed, TRUE MAGICK may not be as simple to practice as you are led to believe; it is not a matter of simply mixing two or three ingredients together and chanting incantations to achieve results. Be careful, this is not how it works, and anyone who tells you otherwise cannot pretend to be a true magician. It takes patience, time and training. Results come with efforts, and they will surely come to whom is willing to work with conscience. Remember that practice makes perfect! And that's how anyone who wishes to reach his goals will be able to cross the finish line. Passion for occultism is a very powerful force. And if this one inhabits you, as I do, then Magick will show itself in its true light and will not fail to amaze you throughout your entire life.

Do you feel attracted and fascinated by dragons? Then, know that Draconia is as powerful as it is exciting; get ready to experience unforgettable moments full of emotions, because that is exactly what awaits you. Its radiance that illuminates us is practically infinite; it vibrates constantly.

Practicing Draconic Magick and working within this knowledge requires cooperation, personal discipline and a deep commitment to be able to rise at a higher level of consciousness and make our dragon friends excellent assistants and co-magicians.

This book, I hope, will restore their glorious reputation and confer them all the honors they have deserved for centuries.

M-A Ricard ~ 555

CAPUT DRACONIS

Head of the Dragon

Draconia versus Wicca

Most of the popular works on Magick today are, more than often, oriented towards the common practices of Wicca, which the vast majority of us simply refer to by the generic designation of *White Magick*.

I believe that a book like this one about High Draconic Magick must demonstrate, first of all, the differences between these two esoteric systems, because for many people, if not a very large majority of the popular mass, the Wicca tradition is perhaps their sole idea of what Magick could be.

I deeply regret the improvisation of some (ignorant) authors who have contributed so much in improperly instructing the pursuers of this Noble Art and all the magicians to be, by revealing to them only very simplified aspects of the Wicca tradition (almost always oriented towards faulty ritual practices), telling their readers that this was the highest form of Magick that exists. It is therefore easy to see why a significant number of neophyte witches think that practicing Magick is nothing else but casting simple spells to obtain power and overcome financial causes, find love, etc. Magick is experienced daily. It is not something that is performed leisurely from time to time.

I do not wish to antagonize some of you, although it may surprise you, but the Wiccan tradition, at least for what we find in books today, is considered *Low Magick*. I'm not telling you to deny Wicca, but just to realize it's only one branch belonging to the tree of the Science of Magick; it is only one of the many aspects of the purest and true Magick.

Although it is possible to draw several parallels or similarities, make no mistake about it. The Magick of Draconic Entities is a science in itself and it could not be seen or considered as a lot of pagan practices that have survived ages and time. Although dragons are noble and magnificent creatures inhabiting the subtle Realms of the Earth since ever, their esoteric teachings are still very little known.

Wicca: Religion of the Earth

The "old religion" is based on the concepts of nature and the Elements that are derived from it. It could be said that the core of Wicca is Mother Earth, Gaïa, the Earth being the plateau on which the forces of the Universe, Sun and Moon, rest and join. This pagan religion, therefore, worships nature, which constantly regenerates itself through the uninterrupted cycle of births, of life and death, to be reborn again.

Mainly based on respect for the Earth and the environment, Wicca saw its admiration decrease over the centuries with the coming of new religions and, above all, because of Christianity. Like most esoteric traditions, Wicca is an art of living, that of coexisting in harmony with the forces of nature.

Wicca also uses a dualistic approach to life and the natural forces it respects. Indeed, this tradition recognizes as supreme power not a single divine source or a single master god-of-all, but rather two well-defined identities (or Entities) personifying the Universal energies: the God and the Goddess, the Sun and the Moon, etc. Witches have always relied on a double force: the God possessing all the attributes of the male current, and the Goddess for her qualities corresponding to the feminine principle. From this cosmogony were born, among other things, the solar and lunar rites and those celebrating the passing of the seasons; the Sabbaths, related to the many beliefs and metaphorical mythology of deities.

Although practitioners of this religion may enjoy working alone, they prefer to group together to form cells known as covens, ideally comprising three to thirteen members who obviously all share the same ideology.

In addition, the Wicca tradition is organized hierarchically; it does not exclude this precept which is found almost within all magickal orders. The leaders of each coven are the high priest and high priestess, thus displaying a fair balance of opposing and complementary forces. Still, duality is once again expressed and omnipresent.

Since this book is not about Wicca practices, for which I have profound respect, what was said will be sufficient to demonstrate what differs from High Magick and the practice of Dragon Magick.

DRACONIA: DRAGON MAGICK

Dragon Magick, commonly known as Draconia or the Draconic Art, is the true science of dragons. Everything that is related to them from near and far comes from the *Draconic Heart*; light source that formed it. It is as old as the dawn of time, always powerful and unique. The foundations of this esoteric system are based on the natural and Cosmic energies found throughout the Universe which vibrate permanently. The signs of this Science of Wisdom can be seen almost everywhere, but it is even easier to find them in quiet places far from human activities, such as parks, lakes, woods and forests, mountains, etc. The closer you are to nature, the better you'll be able to feel the dragons and the splendor of their works.

Draconia is obviously based on the respect for dragons who are its humble emissaries, but it also considers the importance of the elemental and natural energies that collide and unite, and that balance the universal forces governing and constituting our world as it is. From the living beings here below, to the Entities of the Highest Spheres, all play an important role within this beloved Earth, and Draconia recognizes the work of everyone as significant, even essential, for the attainment of the just Equilibrium of the spiritual occult forces of the Cosmos.

The magickal practices resulting from this knowledge are therefore not directed solely for the purpose of increasing in an egoistic way the personal powers of each individual, even though extremely easy to achieve, if such was the wish of the practitioner. Instead, he will have to use his new draconic faculties to elevate himself magickally and spiritually for his own good and that of others. True, Dragon Magick is eminently powerful and great are the achievements that will result on a personal basis, but this power must be used wisely. If not, you might one day receive a violent warning from one of your familiars, making you understand that no! This is not the proper way to go! That would be enough for you to be greatly shaken.

The Dragon path is not an eclectic religion either; it is a very great personal and magickal discipline that requires a deep commitment toward dragons, who will constantly be invoked, and who will work together with the draconic magician. The more noble and valiant he will prove to them, the more favorable and greatly assisting dragons will be.

The practitioner will be able to accomplish real unsuspected wonders. Among other prerogatives, he will be able to communicate with dragons, maintain strong friendships with them and even ride them (see the section of Major Rites) in order to pursue quests in places still unknown today. When the time is right, he will also be allowed to receive important revelations, which to this day have remained hidden from most men. In short, Draconia has many benefits that only a *daraco*[1] will be able to understand, appreciate and use.

That being said, the teachings of Draconia recognize only a sole, indivisible divine source, expressing both male and female principles, perfection, the One. Whether you

---

1   *Daraco*: name given to the Draconic Magician.

call it God, Divine Providence, Universal Light, or Akâsha, it doesn't matter, these names all define the same versatile divine source. In opposite to the Wicca practices, which besides pleading the God and the Goddess (which are initially only figures of the attributes of the same Divine Source) implore a pantheon of deities and various lesser divinities. The draconic magician, for his part, will recognize a single Unique and Primary Force that is above all that exists, and will work together with it and the dragons. He will also address himself directly to the draconic power, the very core of the dragon's life force, and his winged ministers imbued with age-old wisdom and considerable knowledge. He will invoke in due course their unique qualities for all his magickal, occult, spiritual or personal works.

Moreover, Draconia practitioners do not form covens or cells per se, like those found among witches. By far, they prefer to work in solitary and perceive the draconic discipline as a spiritual and individual magickal development, but do not prevent occasional group activities with their companions if desired.

Again, because this esoteric knowledge has just become public[2], we still have a few followers of this unique discipline throughout the world, but we can be sure that in a very near future, we will see rise many more draconic magicians.

This also explains why practitioners of Draconia, although they nonetheless possess personal grades corre-

---

2   Editor's note: This book was first published in 2003. Since then, Draconic Magick has grown incredibly in popularity.

sponding to their magickal development, are not hierar-chical. Only dragons are. Indeed, as for all living creatures and Celestial Spirits, there are within the draconic com-munity different degrees of erudition called the *Chain of Wisdom*. Because dragons are highly knowledgeable about science, including philosophy and Magick, to name a few, they hold what can be called degrees that correspond to the levels of wisdom they possess. The further we go up to the pinnacle of this hierarchy of dragons, up to the Draconic Kings, the higher their level of wisdom and spiri-tual maturity will be.

The magician must also know that this Universal law will also apply to all other Spirits of nature, such as Elementals (Gnomes, Sylphs, Undines and Salamanders). His purpose will therefore be to speak with the kings of each group of entities, if he wishes, to learn everything there is to know about their Elements and their powers. Thus, the pursuers of this noble Art, being Draconia, will notice how beneficial it is in its many aspects and how inti-mately connected it is to the dragons, to nature, the Earth that carries them and to the Universe in all its grandeur and perfection. Putting the teachings of dragons into prac-tice will make every day a great celebration.

THE REVELATIONS OF DRAGONS

L ET no one doubt the existence of dragons! They do exist and will always remain close to us, ready to intervene on behalf of their beloved and faithful companions of the Draconia. Since time immemorial, dragons have been present in the minds of people of different cultures. Sometimes depicted as long winged snakes, sometimes as giant titanic creatures or even as sea serpents, dragons have long been present in our lives, in various forms, sizes and aspects.

These beings possess many characteristics. They appear as imposing guardians of the Great Draconic Knowledge and also as the archetypal personification of strength and power, nobility and wisdom. Dragons have resisted the wear and tear of time and human misconceptions. Stronger than ever at all levels, this is one of the reasons why they symbolize and embody, among other things, psychic regeneration and immortality.

Ever since humans began archiving and keeping records of past events, dragons have been constantly cited. The word dragon comes from the Latin *draco*. In addition to being the name to designate draconic Beings, the term is also employed to express many realities within various sciences such as astronomy, alchemy, astrology, psychology and, of course, Magick.

The constellation of Draco

Furthermore, to return to astronomy, the very long chain of stars located in the celestial north and winding just between Ursa Major and Minor[3] is called the constellation of Draco. It has the characteristic of resembling a winged snake or, rather, evoking a slender dragon body.

---

3   Commonly the Great and Little Bear

In ancient times, Draco played a very significant role because this constellation was the guardian of the (polar) star that never moves. This celestial pole was considered the gateway or threshold between the world of mortals and that of eternal immortality.

Many mystical causes are also related to Draco. Notably, one of the main stars in this constellation, *Thuban*, was, a few thousand years ago, the pole star. The large Egyptian pyramids were consciously designed to be perfectly aligned under this star, so as to enjoy its energetic influences both night and day.

Dragons are not remnants of a remote forgotten past. On the contrary, they are still as current as ever. They are part of the history that was, that is, and that will be...

WHAT DRAGONS ARE AND WHAT THEY DO

First, close all of your old fairy tales and medieval storybooks and put them aside because you won't need them in the future. These reveal some information about dragons, transformed by man and none is really accurate. You must now learn to *unlearn*. It's not as easy as it sounds, but the draconic magician, or daraco, has to discern what is right from wrong. Expect from now on to be thoroughly re-educated.

Dragons possess tremendous powers. One of their many qualities that you must absolutely know —and above all understand— is that they control the elemental energies felt by all living creatures and especially, humans.

The Universe is made up of an amalgam of vibratory frequencies. Everything is pure energy. The denser and slower the vibrations, the closer we get to the raw world of matter. On the other hand, the higher and faster the vibratory rate, the closer we get to the spiritual and divine world. This is why among other realities, there are several planes of existence and why also, some beings live on different levels, in multiple subtle Realms. They don't all vibrate at the same frequency.

Living beings can therefore transmit and extend their energy field into their immediate surroundings and imbue the latter with their feelings, consciousness and purity (or malignant impurity). And it's that radiance, or aura, that dragons and all other entities, easily gather and interpret.

This evidence helps us to understand why draconic Beings are highly suspicious of men. They know us all too well; we have no secrets from them. Men are credulous, impressionable, and capable of dishonesty. They have a constant thirst for power and wealth. Dragons know that humans are too often willing to do anything to achieve their ends, and so, they prefer to withdraw in silence rather than witness awkward and stupid acts on our behalf.

Despite these warnings, which are only directed to those of little faith, once you have succeeded in demonstrating that your intentions towards dragons are pure and righteous, you will be entitled to come into contact with these forces of another dimension. It will be an unparalleled day for you, an event to celebrate, as you will begin to forge powerful bonds with these valiant companions without equal. This will be the beginning of a superb relationship based on friendship and trust with dragons and the draconic world. You will soon realize that they will become not only powerful allies and assistants, but also excellent vigilant protectors. If you believe in them, your attitude will be greatly rewarded.

Dragons, like all creatures and Elementals in the Universe, are entrusted with many daily tasks that they must perform. Their primary mission, valid for all races of dragons whatever they may be, is to stand watch so that the Great Knowledge does not fall into evil hands and dishonest people, hungry for excessive powers, who, through the misuse of this wisdom, could harm and even destroy the just Universal balance between earthly men and Cosmic forces. Even though their work goes unnoticed by most of us, they have very heavy responsibilities and we are all indebted to them for the work they do. Without this support, the world as we know it today would change and be quite different. Everything could become much worse.

In addition of protecting this mystical jewel of Draconia, dragons, depending on their race or draconic type, will also have to perform various tasks suited to the abilities and fields of action, specific to each of the existing classes. By handling energies, they will be active in several domains: terrestrial, psychic and Universal. Each elemental and subtle action has the possibility of being the extension or result of a precise work of a dragon. To learn more about the functions of each race, please refer to the chapter regarding dragon types further in this book.

The Dragon's Lair: The Subtle Planes

There is a widespread belief that dragons are only creatures of the collective imagination conveyed by legends. However, these majestic beings have actually lived among us for a very long time, but somehow, under the seal of secrecy. When we are guardians of a fabulous esoteric treasure, there is no obligation to show it off to anyone. Only egocentric people are capable of such behavior. And in the interest of preserving this treasure and showing great wisdom, dragons have kept silent, for they do not wish in any way to dazzle upon the profane all the knowledge and power they possess. "Step forward and prove your worth!" are words you will hear some day when you take your first steps in Draconic Magick.

Indeed, dragons are extremely clever, and only a person with a pure heart can, with time and patience, gain their trust. Trust is one of the Golden rules of Draconic Magick, as PNFYR once taught me.

Consequently, the reason why so far no one has been able to prove scientifically and with accuracy that dragons really exist, is because these same people have tried in vain to find these beings where they are not! Dragons live on a different plane, a more subtle dimension close to ours: *the higher Realms of the astral plane*. And that explains why, to this day, all have failed in their quest to hunt them down in the depths of their lairs; a piece of knowledge was fortunately missing — dragons are invisible to ordinary people because they have no physical bodies...

Dragons do not inhabit the material world such as humans, animal and the vegetal kingdom do, but they still have well-defined features and appearance. Since their body vibrates at a higher rate than that of matter, as explained above, it cannot therefore be detected by the physical eye. Remember that the laws of time and space have no influence on subtle Beings and dragons. They are not subject to the rules of the material plane. They are omnipresent. With a flapping of wings, so to speak, they can move from one place to another as quickly as the speed of thought.

Views of the Planes of Existence

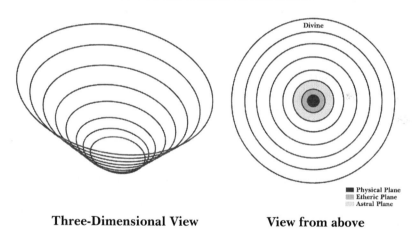

Three-Dimensional View   **View from above**

Of course, these diagrams are a simple visual representations of the planes of existence, used to demonstrate, according to our linear conception, how all are connected to each other by a unique center.

Before discussing these higher zones of the astral, Realms where dragons reside, a more detailed explanation is needed, as many of you still questions the various planes of existence.

The etheric and astral planes are the invisible dimensions closest to the physical world; they are, like all other planes of existence, concentric and *interpenetrate each other*, nested within our material dimension. Imagine, for example, the air that we breathe. You are able to feel a cool breeze on a summer day. However, if the air were also filled with a very volatile gas, you would be unable to see it or detect it, as it would be too subtle to be perceptible but would still be present.

To put it differently, all planes of existence are in the same place, at the same time. They all coexist together at the same time, independently of each other. The physical plane has the lowest vibration rate. Then comes the etheric plane, where Elementals are found, among others: Gnomes, Sylphs, Undines and Salamanders. Next we find the astral which is itself subdivided into multiple sub-planes or various zones of density, including the lower astral, which refers to the Hell of Christianity, the terrestrial or lower astral and the higher astral. The astral plane vibrates at an intensity above the etheric plane. Then comes the mental plane, which vibrates faster than the astral plane and so on, until the perfect spark, the divine dimension.

To illustrate this important concept, imagine the Universe as a staircase that you climb backwards. The bottom of the staircase corresponds to the physical world of matter, our objective world. Always with your back turned to this staircase, climb one step; the latter corresponds to the etheric plane. Go up again to the next step which would be the astral plane. Stop climbing for a while. As you don't see what's behind, by looking down you will be aware of the steps (planes or dimensions) below you. Is this making more sense to you? No matter where you stand (or in what plane of existence you are), you will always be able to perceive the previous steps or, more precisely, *the lower planes*. The higher you are, the more you will be capable to contemplate the many previous planes of existence.

This is obviously a metaphor. Instead of stairs, we refer to these areas in terms of vibratory rate. What vibrates at a higher level (or the steps of our imaginary staircase behind our back) is not, so to speak, perceptible unless one is trained or spiritually elevated. However, all the lower planes (or the steps below us) will be visible to the inhabitants of the higher planes. Since we live incarnate and limited at the bottom of this spiritual chain, at the first step, it is obvious that most humans only perceive what their physical eyes manage to see, nothing more.

THE DRACONIC ZONE

As we have just seen, the Universe is subdivided into various vibratory layers or different levels of consciousness. Some of these layers are also subdivided into several sub-planes, just like a unique world within another that encompasses everything, which itself is part of another, even greater world. Several small Universes within one larger Universe; it's the principle of the microcosm and the macrocosm.

This could look like a multi-story building. Each of these floors, the basement, the ground floor, and so on up to the roof are unique worlds, living in the same building, that is part of a certain city, in some country, etc. This explanation shows how you could represent the astral plane, being divided into multiple zones of density.

The Astral Plane

This dimension contains as many realities as does the earthly plane; it is also populated by several types of inhabitants and Spirits. For example, the lower astral (commonly called Hell) is the most remote and dense place where one would find mainly demons, spectres and devils, and all malignant creatures whose level of consciousness is, in reality, more bestial than human in nature.

In regards of the lower astral, think of a train station; a place where the disembodied or, one might say, the newly deceased are to be found. Of course, like the demons we have just spoken of, do not possess the same degree of spiritual maturity like dragons; they will therefore not reside in the same place, but rather in the darker dimensions, which will be specific to their spiritual degree.

> *It is strongly discouraged for beginners to attempt any contact with the Entities from this level of spiritual consciousness, as they can be extremely dangerous for the inexperienced magician.*

So how can one explain that the draconic Beings, however powerful they may be, live in a plane of evolution which seems, in short, pretty low given their divine nature? This is only a matter of choice. Because the tasks they need to perform must be done from that level of existence. The day dragons will no longer have a purpose near us, when their energetic work towards the planet and its inhabitants will be accomplished and they will have no more ties, they will rise to a higher level of consciousness and leave the high astral Spheres.

Fortunately for all those who respect and love dragons so dearly, this day is still far away. Much remains to be done.

About Physical and Material Manifestations

Many people have a very legitimate question: is it possible to encounter or see a dragon in daylight through our physical eyes, as clearly as one could come across, say, any animal during a stroll in the forest? My guide answers me positively:

"Yes, it is possible, but on extremely rare occasions, for we, dragons, do deem unnecessary to act this way without important, even vital motives, and we have absolutely nothing to prove to men who cannot believe with the heart, refuting the existence of invisible planes because they only take for truth what the eye can see. We have a work to do for the Great Equilibrium of the One, and do it meticulously and consciously. Of course, it pains us to see there are yet too many unconscious people with frail spiritual openness, but we still hope that, one day, they may finally wake up, and who knows, maybe by then we will decide to reveal ourselves..."

In fact, just like Elementals, dragons will only be seen by the psychic eyes. Thus, the magician who will take the time and trouble to make the necessary efforts to train his psychic senses will obtain very great benefits, because he will be able to feel, to see and even to converse directly with them.

A rude person, however, will be unable to find them, no matter where he looks, unless, of course, dragons decide willingly to show themselves physically. But as PNFYR mentioned earlier, this doesn't happen frequently. Dragons prefer to descend into the etheric plane, which makes them much more easily perceptible for those who possess some degree of psychic awareness.

And so, this is how dragons generally unveil themselves to the daraco; by their etheric body, which will have at first an evanescent, diaphanous, substantially aerial shape and appearance, surrounded by a luminous aura. The more accustomed you are to seeing with the mind's eyes, the clearer and more definite their physical form will become. Of course, dragons have the power to materialize and be seen by any if they wish, in case of absolute necessity or, just to please their co-magician daraco. However, remember; being able does not necessarily means... willing!

CHARACTER TRAITS AND BEHAVIOR

Of a benevolent and passive nature, dragons are creatures capable of showing unfailing calm and patience. They all possess in philosophical, magickal, esoteric and spiritual matters, a high degree of erudition corresponding to their age and hierarchical status within the draconic community (grades in Draconia called *vradysconn*). The older and mature a dragon, the wiser and knowledgeable he will be.

While journeying in Draconia, if one of your familiar dragons was unable to properly instruct you on any subject when requested, if he judged it necessary to see such information disclosed to you, then it would be his duty to bring you the competent dragon who would be willing to do so. Your winged companion would then vouch for you and your truthfulness. But for such a thing to happen, you will need to have proven many times over that you are truly trustworthy. Once again, trust and candor reign supreme. No one can fool dragons because they are able to read your aura, your very thoughts and feel everything that is going on inside every living being, and consequently, deep in your soul.

We could say what I have merely described could be seen as a self-defence mechanism of great use to them. Because men are what they are, dragons tend to be fierce and suspicious at first. But over time, the more valiant you are, the easier it will be for you to address them afterwards.

For example a dragon can easily and relentlessly spend several days, weeks, or even years (calculated according to our own linear conception of time) guarding a draconic magician in need, or to work on readjusting and balancing natural and Universal energies and currents. They are, so to speak, outstanding workers. You will soon realize that, if dragons become your allies, great things could be achieved through their help.

Once their work completed, dragons like to take advantage of the time they have to fly here and there, rest and maintain their relationships with draconic magicians. Never underestimate dragons; they are wise and of uncommon intelligence. However, and this applies especially to young dragons, they can also be curious and very mischievous. They tend to look with a watchful eye every action made by their fellow daracos.

When things go well, energetically wise, they relax, then adopt a cheerful attitude and a good mood. Some of

them even have a predilection for playing nasty tricks towards those they love and care. So don't be surprised if, at
some point, your familiar dragons start playing you little
pranks. When allowed, they like to have fun and laugh,
they have a very good sense of humor... well, at least for
dragons!

Dragons also have a strong appeal for magickal rituals,
and, of course, especially for those dedicated to them : draconic ceremonies. The reason is simple. Since they inhabit
the astral plane, equally known as the plane of emotions,
the astral is hence the place where converge all passions,
ardors, desires and feelings projected and felt by men.
Draconic Beings live, feed and work, among other things,
with these energies. Thus, they are extremely sensitive to
vibratory variations and change, whether positive or negative.

However, when a daraco performs a ritual, a strong
dose of energy is then set in motion and radiates from his
magickal temple. So it is not surprising to understand why
certain types of dragons like to gather in masses, standing
very close to where ceremonies take place, either to support the magician in his work, or simply to bathe in this
highly energy-filled atmosphere.

 DRAGON CLASSES AND TYPES

A NYONE wishing to master Draconia must, above all, know its primary subjects, namely, the dragons. Just as for the great Celestial Hierarchy, which consists of Entities of Light, Masters of Ascension, Archangels, Angels, and so on to most dense creatures, there are also several classes or types of dragons, if you will.

The reason why there is not only one kind of dragon, and that they differ from their fellow brethren, is because each race has been assigned special and individual functions, according to the work that must be done. They have therefore, so to speak, adopted the form corresponding to the nature of the energies they must work with. As mentioned earlier, in addition to protecting the mystical Draconia, dragons also have to perform various tasks according to their abilities and field of action, specific to each class. In this sense, just as we find in nature oaks, apple and cherry trees, which, by analogy with dragons, are all fruit trees, everyone has the noble duty of bringing different fruits to the Earth.

Moreover, because the Elements are intimately connected to certain types of dragons, I have therefore found

it necessary to give a brief overview of the elemental qualities and actions, so that you can understand the contextual
meaning of the explanations that will follow with respect
to these various draconic Beings.

The Elements

The Universe, as well as everything contained within,
is the product of the action of the Elements. These primary forces are found everywhere and manifest themselves simultaneously on all planes of existence. They are
Fire, Water, Air and Earth. To these will be added a fifth
one to form this quintessence which is commonly called in
Magick the Element Spirit, Primordial Divine Source or
Akâsha. In ancient Eastern traditions, these Elements are
called the Tattwas, respectively: Waju, Tejas, Apas, Prithivî
and, finally, Akâsha.

These Elements, which constitute the basis of everything
that exists, are bipolar in nature; that is, they have both
positive and negative polarity, active and passive qualities,
constructive and destructive. From this perspective, the
Cosmic Elements are neither good nor bad. They are in a
way crude, neutral and malleable forces. It is only through
the magician's will that these will become good or evil.

Thus, for each elementary kingdom, dragons will possess distinct forms and special powers in addition to certain character traits and attitudes. They will be capable to
influence our personality, behavior and Magick through
the action of the Element specific to them that each and

every one controls. Unlike Elementals (Gnomes, Sylphs, etc.), who by their very nature work on their own behalf, dragons of the Elements will frequently work together to accomplish various and important tasks.

⊕ Akâsha
△ Air
▽ Water
▽ Earth
△ Fire

In addition, these four primordial Elements have been assigned to each cardinal point, the four quarters of the Earth, the four Watchtowers of the magick circles. To the East we find the Air Element with its warm and humid properties. To the South, the Fire Element, which has the particularity of being hot and dry. The cold and wet in the West corresponds to Water, and finally, to the North, the Earth Element, cold and dry. In Kabbalistic Magick, each quarter is under the care of an Archangel: Raphael, Michael, Gabriel and Oriel (sometimes Uriel). However, in Dragon Magick, these same directions are governed by the four Draconic Kings: Sairys, Fafnyr, Naëlyan and Graël.

DRAGONS OF THE ELEMENT OF FIRE

Dragons of the Fire Element belong to the draconic class of fires and braziers. They're associated with the Southern Quarter. They have a rather stocky and imposing body with long thin necks and tails. They spit fire, constantly throwing small jets of flame. These dragons look pretty much alike the Salamanders from this same fiery Element.

Fire dragons are extremely powerful and unpredictable. On many occasions they give the impression of being very severe having a strong temperament. The daraco will experience some difficulties in his early draconic career to work with them, so much their power is difficult to harness. These dragons do not appreciate wasted time and will often show themselves impatient, have a tendency to set fire to everything in their way in order to get things done as quickly as possible, no matter the destruction involved to this end.

Dragons of this Element are governed by the draconic King FAFNYR; he who rules the Southern Quarter. These fiery dragons are found near great fires and braziers, forest fires and, of course, in the very heart of volcanos, all the way down to the magmatic center of the Earth.

On the positive side of the Element from which they come, this race of dragons controls will, strength, power, courage, activity and movement, enthusiasm and determination. They will be of considerable help to develop these qualities effectively and can even clear any obstacles in the way of the practitioner with their powerful breath, just like a volcanic eruption... but at what cost! On the negative side, they also deal with anger and rage, jealousy, hatred and revenge. The draconic magician will therefore have to show discernment if he wants to work on these latter aspects.

Dragons of the Element of Water

Dragons of the Water Element belong to the draconic class of seas and aquatic bodies. They are associated with the Western Quarter. They have a graceful and beautiful appearance and show themselves generally with a long and slender body. Their motion is somewhat like that of large sinuous sea serpents or eels. And just like the latter, with which they share some physical semblance, many watery dragons appear to be without limbs or legs.

Water dragons are calm and composed. From their eyes emanates a strong aura of bliss, wisdom, patience and compassion; as if they could indefinitely remain a passive state . They enjoy the company of draconic magicians and the latter will not fail to invoke them so much their presence is soothing and peaceful. However, if these dragons become upset, they can also be carried away, as abruptly as torrents or in the likeness of waves crashing against rocks.

Water dragons are governed by the draconic King Naëlyan; he who rules the Western Quarter. They are found everywhere where the aqueous Element is expressed, i.e., ponds and lakes, streams and rivers, seas and oceans, etc.

On the positive side of the Element from which they come, this race of dragons controls modesty, fervor, sobriety, love and compassion, peace, tranquility and calm, forgiveness and finesse. They will help the magician to control and better manage his emotions, to make him more magnetic and appreciate the splendor of the Universe. Moreover, it will be possible for him to make things happen in a more fluid way and to breach the barriers of his psyche that holds him back. On the negative side, they also manage indifference, insensitivity, phlegm, condescension, shyness, negligence and inconsistency. Anything that has to do with emotions and water can be the result of the actions of Water dragons.

DRAGONS OF THE ELEMENT OF AIR

Dragons of the Air Element belong to the draconic class of temperature and winds. They are associated with the Eastern Quarter. Very beautiful in appearance, they look pretty much like the Oriental dragons. They usually have a tortuous elongated thin body with remarkably large wings. Some dragons of this species exhibit similar physical characteristics of the Aztec plumed serpent Quetzalcoatl, having bird-like wings of a semblance of feathers.

At first glance, the Eastern dragons will be difficult to befriend and will appear somewhat independent, giving you the impression that they are somehow avoiding you. This should in no way discourage you. Because if you persist, they will come to you and engage communication.

These dragons look constantly in motion, vagabonds, as if they were floating permanently carried by a breeze. Their sinuous bodies swirl around as they move from left to right, as if dancing, their tails gently following this body stream. Slow and graceful, almost hypnotic as their movements can sometimes seem, they also know how to be extremely sharp and fast, breaking the air at lightning speed.

Air dragons are governed by the draconic King SAIRYS; he who rules the Eastern Quarter. Dragons of this Element are usually found in the atmosphere, clouds, hilltops and everywhere in height, where the wind blows.

On the positive side of the Element from which they come, this race of dragons controls intellectual and mental faculties, temperament, joy and pleasure, clarity and vivacity of mind, skill, cordiality and optimistic attitudes. They can be very helpful to the daraco in order to help him increase his creativity, open his mind to new ideas and concepts, etc. On the negative side, they also manage lightness, boasting, chatter, presumptions, dissipation, frivolity, inattention and forgetfulness. These dragons also preside over winds, storms, hurricanes, climate and rain. Be sure that if dragons of this Element are invited when there's a celebration, there will be a lot of fun... in the air!

DRAGONS OF THE ELEMENT OF EARTH

Dragons of the Earth Element belong to the draconic class of plains, woods, forests and rocky mountains. They're associated with the Northern Quarter. Their appearance is pretty much like we regularly see in movies and similar to what Western men have pictured them. They have an imposing body, bearing horns of various sizes, a neck as long as their tails, as well as very large and powerful wings.

Dragons of the Earth are one of the races that remain closest to humans. Because they are intimately connected with nature, which men constantly transforms or, unfortunately, destroy (something that upsets them to the utmost), they keep a watchful eye on us at a distance. The eco-friendly daraco will notice that these dragons are undoubtedly the easiest elemental dragons to approach and will therefore try to communicate with them first, before heading to the other elemental draconic races.

These dragons are under the tutelage of draconic King GRAËL; he who rules the Northern Quarter. Most dragons of this Element are to be found on plains, plateaus and even deserts, in woods and forests, and also in mountains, caves, escarpments and on top of prominent peaks.

From the positive polarity of the Element from which they come, this race of dragons controls all forms of esteem, depth, perseverance, punctuality, temperance and responsibility. They will help you build a solid and sustainable foundation for all the businesses you start throughout your life. These dragons will be of great help in achieving stability, prosperity, endurance and personal strength, etc. From their negative polarity, they also manage laziness and idleness, melancholy, heaviness, irregularity and disloyalty (which they do not appreciate). These dragons also preside over avalanches, landslides, earthquakes and all kinds of ground manifestations.

GREAT WHITE DRAGONS

Great white dragons, commonly called dragons of light, govern the male currents and see the proper balance of elemental forces; Air, Fire, Water and Earth. In Draconia, they manage and rule over the positive energies and polarities of the latter. They are, in a way, the chief leaders of the primary constructive Cosmic energies. These dragons represent the fifth Element of Spirit (on its positive side) located at the top of the pentagram.

These draconic Beings show themselves to the daraco wrapped in a luminous aura. They give the impression of being translucent and their physical features are sometimes difficult to perceive, as if they were only made of strongly compressed light, as if one were looking directly at the sun in broad daylight. They are very similar to the dragons of the Order.

They are found everywhere where light is expressed (physical and Universal), without the existence of darkness. They are hence omnipresent. The qualities associated with White dragons are: Draconia, spirituality, spiritual awakening and elevation, divine Magick, light, the sun, harmony, glory, truth, love, sharing, freedom, goodness in all its forms, indulgence, chivalry, purification of karma, etc.

By invoking these dragons, together with the Great black dragons, the magician will be able, among other things, to manifest his will and balance the flow of elemental energies produced and put it into motion during ceremonies of Dragon Magick.

GREAT BLACK DRAGONS

Great black dragons, also known as shadow dragons, govern the female currents and balance the elemental forces, as do the Light dragons. Within Draconia, they manage and rule over the negative energies and polarities of the Elements. These dragons also represent the counterpart of the Spirit Element (on its negative side), thus forming a perfect unity, the two perfectly balanced currents, transmuted as a unique whole. The Black dragons are, therefore, the complements of the White dragons; they have the same powers and perform the same tasks respectively.

Not in a demonic sense, these very dark dragons have a jet-black body. Just as if they were veiled by the night, which physically expresses their own nature, these creatures are not at all evil nor terrible, quite the contrary. Like their white companions, they are difficult to describe.

Normally, they are detected by a large mass of darkness, such as a gigantic shadow, from which only glowing eyes pierce through darkness.

They are found everywhere where darkness is expressed (physical and subtle), without the existence of light. They, too, are everywhere. The qualities associated with Black dragons are the same as the White dragons, but in their negative forms: misused Draconia, density, fears, sleep and spiritual regression, harmful Magick, darkness, the moon, conflict, losses, lies, despotism, heavier karmic debts, etc.

An important clarification is now required. Know that the Great black dragons do not work for evil and that a malicious practitioner will never be able to satisfy his egoistic desire for revenge through their interventions. In the Draconic Science, using words like darkness and blackness does not necessarily express human concepts of evil as opposed to good.

Now, since the Cosmic Elements are all bipolar by nature, one negative side and one positive, one cannot exist without the other. The representation of Yin and Yang perfectly demonstrates the relationship between White and Black dragons. It will be obvious that everything is a question of balancing Universal energies and never about black Magick.

DRAGONS OF THE ORDER

Dragons of the Order are the draconic creatures that watch over the cycles of rebirths and the restructuring of beneficial energies. They work together with the dragons of Chaos, who must destroy everything and bring death to discordant currents, so that dragons of the Order can subsequently relieve them from their duties and take over the rebuilt of everything on a new, more solid and positive basis.

In other words, if there were, figuratively speaking, a ruined castle inhabited by specters that would only bring fear and desolation, dragons of Chaos would be the ones entrusted with the task of bringing it down in pieces, so that the dragons of the Order could then rebuild it into a real fortress, ready to welcome new and pure tenants.

Therefore, their job is to watch over order and balance, to start all over again from scratch, and to bloom harmonious seeds. When there are big disruptions, which will inevitably be resolved by huge changes, you can be certain that dragons of the Order will be nearby. They will be on the lookout, patiently waiting in silence for their turn to arrive and take charge of the events.

To see the presence of a dragon of the Order usually means wonderful things are about to happen, to be born, or that he simply ensures that everything is going well, and that men, daracos and the Earth are okay, like a father watching over his children.

The magickal possibilities offered by these draconic Beings will help you stabilize or start new projects, work on your personal relationships, improve all situations, even lost or desperate causes, by giving rise to feelings of hope and the energy required to go through trials. In addition, you will have the opportunity to find along the way the tools needed that will allow you to move forward. Thanks to the support of these dragons, you will be able to rise from your ashes just like a phoenix.

DRAGONS OF CHAOS

Dragons of Chaos, also known as Chaotic dragons, are the creatures with the most impressive stature of all Draconia. They have large and powerful wings in addition to a massive dark body. They look as if darkened by a moonless night or better yet, like if they were actually overshadowing everything, standing tall and gigantic, their broad wings outstretched. They are very similar to the Great black dragons, with whom they share some physical similarities, but Chaotic dragons would appear somewhat at least twice in size.

Their work consists, not in a negative way, in destroying wrong creations, only to rebuild them better afterwards, thanks to the intervention of the dragons of the Order. Sometimes it is better to undo everything and start over, rather than to put splints that will eventually yield. Thus, just as for the Earth life cycles, which are reflected in the perpetual circle of birth, life, death and rebirth, their functions will be to eliminate and bring to an end bad energies and make room for renewal, and help recreating pure new and solid energetic bases.

Dragons of Chaos act quickly with great efficiency, in a drastic and fatal way that no one can conceive; but in no way will they be considered demonic or evil.

Their presence is frequently seen as a bad omen, because they are usually found where is disasters, such as earthquakes, volcanic eruptions, storms and hurricanes, tidal waves, and floods. It is therefore not surprising to understand the link between the different types of dragons. The dragons of Chaos can be seen in the company of the Fire dragons during forest fires, with the dragons of the Order ready to take over. They are behind the Water dragons when the sea becomes extremely rough, etc.

Although death and rebirth are hence associated with Chaotic dragons, their magickal power must not be rejected by any draconic magician. It's even very important to him and of extreme significance. It is only when the daraco understands this force as being neither bad or evil, and necessary for renewal, being properly prepared to meet these powerful dragons, will he then be able to call them forth and work with them to produce great changes in his life, and to the very depths of his soul. However, meticulous care will have to be taken when the terrible dragons of Chaos are used in magickal ceremonies. In fact, just as like Fire dragons, the changes brought by these Beings are carried out in a direct and instantaneous manner and sometimes even without warning, with a power such as an unmerciful sword thrusted into the enemy.

Familiar Dragons

Familiar dragons will probably be the ones you'll work with most frequently. These dragons are undoubtedly the closest to the daraco. Their appearance is very diverse and so is their size. They can be as massive and imposing as an elephant, as well as small, no more than the size of a cat.

Once you have started to walk the path of Dragon Magick, you will be able to perform the ritual of calling on the protective familiar dragons. This ritual will consist of asking to be assigned one or even several dragons to watch over you and your home. You will notice in a very short time that their help will be most valuable and very profitable.

These familiar dragons are the friendliest of all the Draconia. The reason is simple; since they will have to spend the vast majority of their time with you, as if they were in a training course in the human race, in order to increase their occult powers, you will have the chance to forge powerful friendships with them. True, it is possible to have this class of guardians at one's disposal without having to worry about them. However, it is highly recommended to take the time to give them love and care. If your familiar dragons feel the emotions you have for them, they will hold on to you and become true comrades. They will even be overprotective in some respects, without hesitating to run at your rescue in dangerous situations or to impose themselves strongly between you and threatening people, by opening wide their wings and making grunts to shake the Earth...

These guardian dragons are also playful, curious, and sometimes even funny to watch. They like to stand close to the draconic magician whom they protect in order to observe him in his mundane actions, at times leaning over his shoulder when he writes, occasionally perched on a library to get a good overview of what is happening. They get along pretty well with the other inhabitants of the house and pets, and sometimes even start chasing them for the pleasure of playing. Indeed, it is not uncommon to see this attitude full of humor, especially among the smaller and younger dragons who seem to enjoy playing tricks. Older dragons, on the other hand, will be wiser and much quieter.

Familiar dragons also love to watch the daraco performing his rituals. They carefully study all his actions until the closing of ceremonies of Draconia. You can expect your familiar dragons to help you in your magickal workings for protection, of course, in addition to love and friendship, divination, development of psychic powers, etc. These dragons have knowledge in many areas, but at times, depending on their age and maturity, slightly below that of other dragons who might prove more qualified.

In short, familiar dragons are great, loyal friends; the more attention and affection you give to them, the more will they reciprocate. Over time, you will simply become inseparable!

CORPUS DRACONIS

Body of the Dragon

THE FIRST STEPS: QUESTING FOR DRAGONS

Now that you are firmly determined to take the path of Dragon Magick and follow their occult teachings; because you feel more than ever this attraction toward Draconia and want to be in the ever company of draconic creatures, even fly with them (and you'll see that this is possible), perhaps you are wondering where to find these precious magician's assistants and how to contact them?

Know that, from the moment you think about them, as you read those lines, they hear your thoughts. If they think of you, they will be with you. Dragons are everywhere, all around us, but normally we just don't see them. Maybe there's one standing right behind you, but unaware for now, you're not yet able to perceive or feel him. If such is the case, worry not, because you will in due time!

Thought and State of Mind

Dragons tend to dwell where their inner nature is expressed. They enjoy places that evoke their own identity. In that, the magician will visit and explore such areas where are bodies of water to get closer to the dragons of the seas and aquatic bodies. Dragons of the forests will be easier to access near the woodlands and in the wilderness where reigns the Earth Element, etc. Of course, you will easily be able to contact these draconic Beings in your magickal temple, without the need to go outside, because remember, dragons are not physical creatures, therefore they can be everywhere, that is to say, they are omnipresent. Furthermore, if you wish to directly contact dragons in their respective habitats, you will simply have to head to these places by traveling through the mind. Thereby, Fire dragons living at the very bottom of volcanos will suddenly become very accessible.

However, opt for solitary places, which are not very busy and remote, where few people dare to venture. Do not force or avidly seek draconic signs when you are in your early daraco career. A maxim reads: when the student is ready, the teacher will appear. This is also true of dragons. Pursue your magickal training in Draconia and when you are ready to meet them, even if without your knowledge dragons have often been present in your surroundings, then will they decide, of their own accord, to slowly unveil themselves and appear to you in all their splendor.

Remain passive and observe in silence, in recollection,

and above all, in the love of these draconic Beings. Pay attention to all the little things that usually elude you: a whisper in the wind, a stealthy shadow, a rustle of leaves or branches. And most importantly, relearn what we call child's wonder.

This meditative state suggests you break your shackles created by the rational world, that you accept your great power of imagination, for it will allow the emergence of the highest faculties of intuition and inspiration in human beings. It is these same faculties, these innate gifts, that connect us to the subtle worlds, that open the way to vision and spiritual awareness.

GIVE AND YOU WILL RECEIVE

When we want to follow the draconic path, we must first be ready for change and expect to see transformations taking place in ourselves and all around us. Draconia is a science that requires patience, effort, deep commitment and personal discipline, aimed at nothing but magickal and spiritual improvement. The magician must know nothing happens without a reason, but moreover, that dragons, despite the delicate attention they are capable of, will give nothing without getting something in return.

They do not seek rewards, quite the contrary! You'll win all the honors because of them. Yes, it's a fact, dragons will always ask an offering for services rendered. On the other hand, what they ask in return will not be such as *"give me something and only then I shall give you"*, but rather

"I am ready to help you but first, show me you wish to make the necessary efforts to improve your situation..."

Do you understand what dragons want from you? It's not a material offering or worse, a sacrifice. No, they just want you to improve yourself spiritually and magickally, to do good around you and for yourself! There is an adage that says: Heaven helps those who help themselves. Well, that couldn't be truer: *Help yourself and the Draconia will help you in return.*

Are you surprised that dragons do not ask for more? What they expect is really very little if we understand that we should all aim for such goals, even if Magick was totally unknown to us! And so goes the exchange between the practitioner and dragons. By working on yourself, by following this draconic magickal training, you will deploy a great force provided with energies that will be felt and absorbed by all dragons. This force that will radiate through you (and you will see that it is very easy to do), in conjunction with beneficial thoughts, will feed the powers of dragons. In short, aspire to noble goals and the draconic Beings will reward you a *hundredfold*. You have everything to gain.

THE FIRST CONTACT

You may be very surprised the first time you look at a real dragon, standing right in front of you. They are used to being quiet and silent the first time they are seen by a daraco. The dragon facing you will remain impassive, at first, observing you for a moment. While breathing very slowly and deeply, his breath will caress you with a gentle intoxicating warmth.

His gaze will be extremely penetrating and full of wisdom, to such an extent that you will feel he has the power to probe the very depths of your soul (most likely, that's exactly what he will do). And because they are capable to see and feel the energies you project, what is happening inside you, your inmost feelings and thoughts, but above all, what's in your heart, it will be more than likely that you will be unable to react at this first encounter, so much so you will have this feeling of bliss, as if you were bathing in an ocean of light and truth.

It even happens that, overwhelmed by this unique moment of greatness and magnificence within this new, almost indescribable bond, between this draconic Being and yourself, you come to shed a few tears.

This calm face, expressing such great goodness will mark you forever, rest assured. After several minutes have elapsed; the dragon will finally take a step forward and address you by telepathy, their preferred way of communication. What he tells you next will depend on the dragon, you and your goals in Draconic Magick. One thing is for sure, this will be an important and especially unforgettable moment.

It is also possible, during this first encounter, that your dragon will reveal very little to you, not even its name. Perhaps it will be for later, at a future meeting, which will certainly not be long in coming. Remember, dragons will take all the time they need to know you, without haste. Stay pure, good and patient; it is well worth it.

THE DRACONIC MAGICIAN: THE DARACO

T HE magician who practices the teachings of Draconia is called a *Daraco*. He is the one who studies the Spiritual Knowledge and Dragons' High Magick. He knows the techniques to connect with the Draconic Force and knows how to use it to express his will on the material plane, through the dragons, who are his powerful allies.

If in your magickal and spiritual quest you find the dragon path being an excellent way to achieve your personal fulfillment, not to mention the immense joy you will experience in working closely with these draconic Entities, then know that there are some points to consider. Although these are within everyone's reach, that is, you have this potential within yourself, it is still imperative it appeals to you, otherwise you will find it difficult to excel in Draconic Magick.

In addition to the qualities required for the conduct of the daraco, which are clearly expressed in the Draconic Code, you must of course love dragons deeply and recognize their effectiveness, that goes without saying! If they don't feel this bond of complicity, they will more likely avoid your company than respond to your calls. Dragons don't like being around mean, rude people.

And you need to be able to rely entirely on dragons. In other words, your faith in them must be unshakable. Know that their powers are immense and that a magician who binds with them will be rewarded with a very powerful force. Having said that, you must have no doubt in your mind when you perform Dragon Magick, *for to doubt is to fail*. Know how to recognize this great power that inhabits you, this magickal and spiritual force. Know your potential. Trust yourself, but above all, have trust in dragons.

Ultimately, always work for good and never for the ruin of others. A draconic magician is noble, and his behavior is reflected by his way of thinking and how he sees the Universe in which he interacts. There is always a way around even the most difficult problems without ever wishing anyone harm. Never attempt to control a dragon to attack someone else, even if you think that's the only way to go. Sooner or later, dragons will show you the uselessness of such actions, in an extremely clear way.

THE DRACONIC CODE

DRACONIA is not intended to be dogmatic and will never exert any form of pressure on anyone. Only beings capable of capturing the appeal for this High Science will be able to follow the draconic path. We all have free will, and therefore the choice to follow this precious teaching with joy and passion or to close this book; to accept the truths presented here or to reject them; to engage and develop magickally and spiritually or to remain weary and idle.

On the other hand, for all those who wish to follow the draconic practices ardently and work in complicity with dragons, know that within this hermetic science, there is a type of code of chivalry that can be know as ethics or Golden rules. This code is scrupulously applied by all dragons. They will demand the same for you if you decide to follow in their footsteps on their path. Any serious daraco apprentice must take the time necessary to study these rules and understand them, or even learn them by heart. Later, he will apply them throughout his life. There is no doubt great benefits awaits you through these.

The Draconic Code consists of the following eleven Golden rules:

I. — Deep Respect of Dragons

Draconic Entities and all Draconia Beings are to be respected in all circumstances, as well as for the works they perform, whether visibly or invisibly, on this plane of existence or another, in this life or in another. Dragons are Beings of rare erudition. Their advice demonstrates great and profound wisdom. They are allies of the daraco and you must treat them as your equals.

II. — Respect for Universal Creatures

The daraco recognizes that he is not the master of the Earth, but rather that he coexists in harmony with all Universal creatures. From dragons to men, from animals to trees, from plants to stones; all play a significant role within the balance of the One. Every action, big or small, affects another, and we are all connected to each other. Size, look and shape don't matter; all living creatures have their unique purpose.

III. — Free will and Freedom of Choice

We all have free will, and that freedom allows us to choose what feels right and appropriate to us, even if later those choices turn out to be wrong or negative. Choosing means it is possible to make mistakes, and through these, great life lessons can be learned. Draconia is a science and a way of life working along Universal Energies, but it should not be seen as the only path to follow, nor will it be presented as such. Several paths lead to the top of a mountain and everyone has the right to take their own trail with regard to opinions, beliefs, religions or codes of conduct.

IV. — Know Thyself

We have to learn what our capabilities and our limitations are. Recognizing ignorance is the beginning of knowledge. Learning to know oneself is the primary basis for perfecting one's knowledge, obtaining self-respect and from others, as well as spiritual upliftment and Draconic enlightenment. It also means we must be able to exercise good judgment and listen attentively to our intuition, as well as to our heart.

V. — Value and Trust

Fairness, honesty and loyalty will be part of the vital principles of the daraco. By expressing these qualities, he will gain not only the trust of dragons, but also that of his peers. Trust implies we are worthy and that our actions express a chivalrous attitude. The sharing of the High Draconic Knowledge is performed on the basis of these principles and the confidence that one acquires. This quality being recognized, dragons will accept the daraco with dignity as one of their own.

VI. — Act with Consciousness

Just as dragons are sentient Beings, every action and ritual should be performed with this in mind. Dragon Magick must be practiced seriously and each magickal action should never be undertaken lightly, because the force drawn from within Draconia, is of such power, that it would be possible to wreak havoc from a misuse of Draconic energies. This rule is closely related to the tenth rule of the Code.

VII. — Meditate and Converse

To meditate and converse with dragons is the way by which information is exchanged with magicians. Many messages are communicated during meditation sessions. To center oneself in silence, recollection and passivity will make it possible to perceive and obtain, sometimes even extraordinary, visions of things past, present or to come. Dragons use this language of communication mainly and almost exclusively. Meditation will therefore bring the daraco the necessary level of elevation, thus allowing familiar dragons or any other Draconic Being to converse directly with him in order to share information.

VIII. — Invoke Often

Dragons know how to listen to draconic magicians who have forged special bonds with them. *Invoke your winged assistants, invoke them often!* He who never asks for anything will never receive anything. On the other hand, whoever asks for the dragons' help and invokes them will be heard and even answered, provided that his requests are just and valid and do not contradict the laws that govern the Universe. A daraco will never underestimate dragons because he recognizes their remarkable qualities, their might and the help he is able to receive from them.

IX. — The Science of Goodness

Draconia is, above all, the ultimate knowledge and power of dragons. This esoteric science is oriented mainly towards knowledge, personal development and magickal practices, goodness, action of elementary energies and defense. It is never employed for provocation or direct magickal attacks. Sometimes, and on rare occasions, an attack may seem like the best defense you have. But that depends on the circumstances. At that point, the judgment will be questioned. It is imperative that the daraco comply with this rule, otherwise he may lose the draconic guides and assistants he has been granted.

X. — Mastering Draconia

Mastering the microcosm to make changes within the macrocosm means being able to control yourself and achieve mastery of one's self. Mastery is the ultimate path to follow when one profoundly seeks external results through Dragon Magick. Controlling our own small universe, in order to bring about change within the Great Universe, is to understand and effectively apply the principles of Draconia that will make the daraco a respected and powerful draconic magician.

XI. — Preserving and Teaching Draconia

It is the daraco's duty to preserve first and foremost the draconic heritage and to pass it on to his relatives who share the same love for the dragons, and in whom he has complete confidence. By keeping this precious knowledge intact, which has resisted the erosion of time so well, Draconia will continue to radiate and illuminate the hearts of all practitioners of this marvelous discipline and esoteric tradition for centuries to come.

# Tools of Dragon Magick

T HE authentic mage knows he does not really need to use particular tools during his daily routines of Magick. He recognizes his own inner power, creative visualization and will as being sufficient; these have been properly trained through rigorous exercises and Magick training techniques. He needs nothing else. *He is able to practice Magick with his bare hands.*

However, it should be noted that rituals of ceremonial dragon Magick will still require the use of certain instruments to perfect the practices of Draconia.

The draconic magician's arsenal is composed of several instruments of the Art, also called magickal or ceremonial tools. They each have a particular use and a very precise symbolism in order to control the different elemental and Cosmic forces awakened during the Major Rites. Draconic tools represent the extension of the magician's will, and through them you will be able to skillfully direct the occult and elemental currents you evoke.

The Ceremonial Sword / Draconic Dagger

The ceremonial sword is the main instrument of Draconic Magick. It is the most widely used tool and that's why you should pay special attention to it. The sword has always been the knights noble weapon, and especially of the daracos.

The sword is used when strength is required but more primarily, to banish and guard against invisible and negative forces, as a protective weapon against astral Entities. For this reason, this tool is associated with the Sephirah of Geburah and the planet Mars. Among other uses, it is also handled during evocations and consecrations, to trace pentagrams and magickal symbols, as well as protection circles and to direct energies flowing from the Draconic Force.

It is associated primarily with the Element of Fire, expressing the authority and strength of the will, but also with Air. This paradox is explained by the fact that since the ritual dagger is related to the Air Element, it is normal to consider the sword as a large dagger, and therefore, of the same Element. If you associate it with this Cosmic Element, that is just as well, as long as everything is clear in your mind.

On the other hand, it is certain that a real sword is rather expensive. Also, if your budget does not allow you to get one at the moment, there will always be a way to temporarily bypass the situation and replace it with a dagger, which I recommend or, again, use a sword you will have crafted yourself, the which will still possess all the same occult characteristics. However, it would be better if you considered acquiring a real sword in the near future.

To make your own sword for ceremonial use, there are two options. First, you can buy a long thin steel plate and saw it the size that suits you. Then, you need to shape one end so that it becomes very sharp. The edges of the blade need not to be sharpened. Make a handle with an insulating material and cover it with a material of your choice, such as canvas or leather. All that remains is to draw the characters and symbols in black or white.

The second way is even easier to achieve. Obtain any wooden dowel or other insulating material, about 50-70 cm long and enclose a long, pointed nail, as a blade tip at one end. This technique, although somewhat bizarre, will achieve the same effects due to the qualities of the metal tip and its effectiveness on the astro-electrical fluids of the etheric and astral planes. Finalize it all by painting or etching the magickal symbols.

Symbols and Character of the Ceremonial Sword

The Earth Pentacle

The pentacle is of the Earth Element. Its primary function is to store and redirect the elemental energies of the Earth and dragons of the same Element, while also being a balancing agent of the other elemental energies (Fire, Air, Water). The pentacle alone can be used, among other things, to center yourself when feeling unbalanced, as well as to ward off bad energetic vibrations in order to expel them away from your immediate surroundings.

This tool is usually made of wood. Some practitioners will use a flat disk, while others, of a slightly concave form. There are many ways to make a pentacle. You can follow the style of the Order of the Golden Dawn, which consist in dividing the disk into four equal parts and paint it black, olive, rust and citrine. A hexagram in the center of a circle should be drawn in white, while the symbols in black.

To make a pentacle in its simplest expression, take a wooden disk and paint it with black, olive, rust or citrine paint. Alternatively, use the four colors as explained above. Then carefully draw a pentagram inside a circle with white paint or in earthy tones.

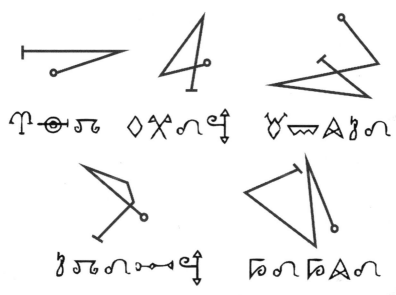

Symbols and Characters of the Earth Pentacle

Finally, on the outline, paint the draconic seals and symbols of the pentacle. Their meaning, as for all the other tools of Art, are as follows:

1- The Greater Divine Name (in three parts) associated with this Element

2- The name of the Draconic King who governs this Elemental Quarter

3- The name of the Cosmic Element

To protect your magickal tools, I recommend that you apply a fine coat of varnish.

The Air Dagger

This dagger does not have the same meaning as the Draconic Dagger, which is used in the same way as the ceremonial sword. This tool is of the Air Element. Its main function will be to redirect and work the airy elemental energies as well as Air dragons.

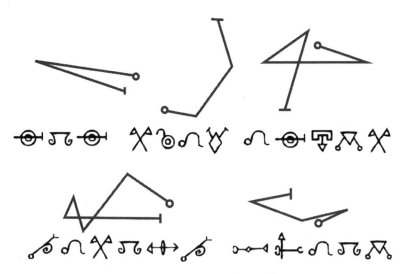

Symbols and Characters of the Air Dagger

To make this draconic tool, acquire a single double-edged dagger with a small T-shaped guard. The handle can be made of any material (preferably wood), as long as this material can easily allow painting. Gently sand the handle of your knife and coat it with one or more layers of bright yellow paint. Then, when the handle is dry, paint the magickal seals and symbols of the Air Element in very bright purple. Finally, coat a thin layer of protective varnish.

THE WATER CUP

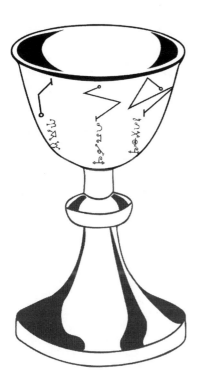

This cup represents the Cosmic Element of Water. It is used during rituals to store, work and direct the elemental energies of Water and dragons of the watery Element.

Crafting the elemental cup can be complex or very rudimentary, depending on your personal taste as a draconic magician.

To achieve a suitable cup, you can take any wooden, metal or glass chalice and cover it (only on the outside) with a good layer of blue paint. Then skillfully draw the seals and draconic symbols corresponding to the Cosmic Element of Water with a very bright orange paint. Complete your work with a final coat of varnish.

If desired, it is also possible to preserve the natural appearance of your cup and only paint the magickal symbols. If you choose that path, then be aware that the seals must be painted blue, while the draconic characters will be orange.

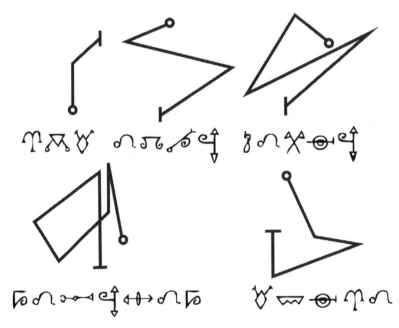

Symbols and Characters of the Water Cup

The Fire Wand

Although there are many types of magick wands, this one belongs to the Fire Element. It will be used to store and redirect fiery elemental energies and those of the Fire dragons. It also represents the magician's all-powerful will.

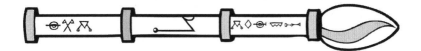

The Fire Wand is of rather a simple construction, especially if you are skilled at working with wood. Use a dowel that will be about the size of your forearm and give it a phallic shape. The circumference is left to your discretion.

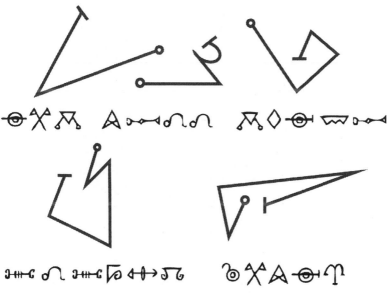

Symbols and Characters of the Fire Wand

Simply choose the size that will give you a good grip. Then apply a red layer (or several if necessary) over its entire area. Finally, mark the draconic symbols with very bright green paint; green is the complementary color here. If desired, to bring more force to your wand, insert a thin magnetized metal wire in the center, along its entire length, from where the north pole will be oriented towards the acorn-shaped end. Complete the manufacture of your wand with a thin protective layer of varnish.

THE DRACONIC PENTACLE

The Draconic Pentacle is of the Element of Spirit. It is used in Dragon Magick rituals to express the daraco's authority to call upon the Draconic Force.

In addition, it symbolizes, in a concrete way, the unity of the Universal Cosmic forces, the balance of energies and the focal point where they all harmoniously converge to become One.

This pentacle can be constructed in the same way as the Earth tool, using identical materials and colors, or, by using a laminated image, always on a wooden disk. However, remember that this instrument of the Art should bear one or two dragon effigies.

Those skilled in High and Ceremonial Magick will understand that the Draconic Pentacle acts in the same way as the Enochian Tablet of Union.

THE RESERVOIR OF DRACONIC POWER

The Major Rites, in Draconic Magick, make use of

two very distinct cups. The first is commonly called the *Draconic Reservoir of Knowledge* or the *Power Chalice*. As its name indicates, this cup will contain the *symbolic blood* (red wine) as well as all the energies graced by dragons during rituals, which will be transmitted to you when you drink its contents at the closing of ceremonies.

This instrument of Dragon Magick is therefore more than essential. This chalice can be made of any material, provided that it is not porous or dangerous. It should rest in the center of your altar during each ritual.

"Power Chalice, Draconic Reservoir of Knowledge, transfer the Wisdom and Light poured by Dragons unto the daraco who drinks you!"

THE MAGICKAL DIARY

The last tool you will inevitably need, and not the least because of its importance, is the grimoire. It is the daraco's log book, its *aide-mémoire*, where all personal notes and rituals can be transcribed.

This magick book is for you only. So, write it in the way you think is most appropriate. One of the recommended uses is to write down all the results of your magick training and draconic ceremonies. In this way, you will be able to see over time how fast you are progressing and under what circumstances you have achieved good (or bad) successes. In addition, you will be capable to devote a number of pages to record all your meditations and

conversations with dragons (and information revealed to you), your draconic quests, Initiation Rites as well as the names and functions of your dragon assistants, whom you will have met during your journeys on the path of High Draconia.

DRAGON'S BLOOD

Dragon's blood incense, mainly in the form of pure resin burned on charcoal, is an excellent magickal agent to be used during rites of Draconia. Dragons (and especially Fire dragons) will delight themselves in this type of fumigation.

Yes, your are right, the simple name of this incense is very evocative, but the fact remains that this resin is excellent for rituals of purification, strength and protection. Dragon's blood is an excellent choice for the magician, whether performing Dragon Magick or not.

That being said, you do not have to stop there. You can, of course, use the fumigations and resins of your choice. If you can't get dragon's blood, then I recommend the use of Frankincense, which has equivalent properties.

And this concludes the chapter on basic tools of Draconia. It is true, there are some other magickal instruments to work with dragons, including more elaborate draconic staffs or wands, but the ones presented here will be most often used, at least for the time being, until you reach a higher level in the *vradysconns*.

Initiation Degrees

T HERE are several levels of initiation to Draconic Magick, six to be more precise. Each of these degrees relates to a step that the magician has taken on his path of improvement. These ranks bear the same name as those of dragons, namely the *vradysconns*. They all correspond to a different degree of initiation and to a Cosmic Element.

Remember, I mentioned earlier that only dragons are hierarchical. These ranks do not have the function of granting you any superiority over another daraco magician; they are for you only, as personal guides. They are therefore used to make you recognized for your spiritual maturity within the brotherhood of dragons. Like a draconic barometer, showing your progress and the magickal journey you've traveled since you started.

That being said, the way of acquiring draconic degrees will always be done in solitary, by a journey of the mind in the Draconic Zone, a rite consisting of meditations and visualizations. You will not need any help from a third party, or even a more experienced daraco. You, alone, will be both the initiate and your own master. The only prerequisite is to remain honest with yourself, because if dragons deem it necessary to refuse you a higher degree, it is because they have very good reasons to do so and you will have to accept it humbly, so please trust them. Work more on yourself before trying the rite again. Maybe next time will be the right one.

Chart of Vradysconns

Degrees	Elements	Draconic Ranks
First Initiation Degree		Daraco Neophyte
Second Initiation Degree	▽	Paetryn Daraco
Third Initiation Degree	△	Aether Daraco
Fourth Initiation Degree	▽	Stellae Daraco
Fifth Initiation Degree	△	Ignys Daraco
Sixth Initiation Degree	✴	Mytrae Daraco

The first degree ritual is often referred to as *Entering the Dragon's Lair.* This means you will present yourself in the depths of their sanctuary, pure of heart, and ask to be accepted as a draconic magician. It will also be the point of no return, because once in the lair, if you are not fully prepared, you will be denied access and need to leave the premises immediately. On the other hand, if you succeed in this initiatory rite and have proved yourself, you will then be a true daraco (at the rank of neophyte), recognized by the whole brotherhood of draconic Beings.

You will also find in this book the second and third initiatory rite of the Draconia. When you feel ready to move on to a higher level, you could then practice these rituals to obtain respectively the degrees of *Paetryn* and *Aether Daraco*. Once again, I must point out to you that success in Magick is not a race. Mastery is achieved with patience and practice. Go at your own pace, whatever it is, but remain constant. There is no point in trying to burn the steps, otherwise you risk consuming your own expectations and hopes for success. Slowly but surely and everything in due time. Apply this rule and I promise you that your magickal and draconic journey will be crowned with success.

Basic Training of the Draconic Magician

I N addition to daily dragon ceremonies and rituals, if you want to achieve breakthrough results, and eventually become a powerful daraco magician, you should devote some of your time and follow a basic Magick training, and practice it as often as you can.

This magickal draconic training will make you a much stronger and more experienced magician. Among other things, you will be able to permanently draw the Draconic Force in your home, bathe in this benevolent energy, spiritually align yourself with the vibratory frequency of dragons, sharpen your psychic senses so as to develop clairvoyance, and at the same time, perceive more easily the draconic Beings, thus facilitating your exchange with them. All the magickal rituals you will undertake in the future will become more effective and powerful. You will also be able to feel and see things that are still unsuspected to this day, and much more. Major Rituals will bring you great benefits, but add to that the personal development exercises that have been passed on to you by dragons and you truly have a winning strategy.

If you already possess some knowledge of Magick and are currently undergoing some kind of magickal training, the one that follows might be just as beneficial to you. Feel free to mix the practices of this chapter into your actual training. Moreover, know that dragons could easily have transmitted to us an entire work oriented solely to the methods of improvement of the magician. It is in this perspective you should know that the following magickal practices are basic techniques, whose purpose is to position you on the right track. Any other procedure you consider appropriate can also be practiced, depending on your abilities and degree of improvement.

Once you've mastered these Magick exercises, practicing them one at a time, doesn't mean you should stop doing them! Remember that just like a muscle in the human body, even at its best, gradually, over time, it will eventually become heavier and lose its tone if it's not regularly put to exercise...

Draconic Temple Dedication

When you begin the true teachings of Draconia, one of the first things you should do is to dedicate a special place where you'll practice your Dragon Magick. Obviously, the ideal would be to have a room entirely dedicated to your work. Thus, the latter would never be *polluted* by any discordant energies of mundane life.

However, since it is not always possible to own such a magickal temple, once you have determined where most of your ritual and daily practices will be held, organize yourself so that you are comfortable during your training periods. You can, for example, clean a corner of a bedroom and place your altar there, slightly reorganizing the furniture to gain a little extra space to trace the Magick circles, etc. A draconic temple will always remain something very personal. There is, therefore, no rule to follow, except that of preparing and decorating a nice place, which will be clean, suitable and pleasant, and above all, welcoming for the dragons.

*
**

DAILY DRAGON INVOCATION

Here is a very simple ritual that you will perform every day, preferably when you get up in the morning. It won't take you more than a few seconds to practice. It is an invocation, a prayer in a way, that you will address to the Draconic Force in order to strengthen the bond that unites you in Draconia. This invocation is used to raise yourself and adjust your vibratory field and position you at the same frequency as of the dragons.

In other words, this daily statement will attune yourself with the draconic Beings. Remember you can also pronounce it just before you retire for the night; it's even a great idea. Once you have completed this invocation, you will ritually conclude by giving the Triple Sign, explained after.

Put your right hand on your heart and say in a clear voice:

Awake, O noble and mighty Draconic Force,
Awake in me and shine through my whole being!
O breath of Dragons, Great and Wise,
Make my spirit a vessel of Truth.
Offer me your Knowledge and Wisdom,
And teach me the Mysteries of your Magick.
I welcome all the Dragons in my heart and soul,
And may we work together for Draconia!
Bless me among yours,
And lead me to perfection.
O noble Draconic Force, omnipotent Dragons,
Manifest yourself in me and radiate through my being!
Manifest, manifest, manifest!
Shine, shine, shine!
Draconis, draconis, draconis!

Give the Triple Sign.

*
**

THE TRIPLE SIGN

The Triple Sign is a very noble magickal gesture that is given solemnly, with dignity and respect. This is a special ritual greeting. It is thus performed with the right hand, which remains open, fingers joined together:

- Touch your forehead.
- Then touch your heart (or lips).
- Finally, open the arm slowly outward, palm up.

I have noticed over the years that I was unconsciously practicing the Triple Sign in a slightly different way. I have never thought changing this habit, as I find it is quite suitable, if not better. My personal way is as follows:

- Touch your forehead with your right hand.
- Then touch your lips.
- Then touch your heart.
- Finally, open the arm slowly outward.

There are two reasons for giving the Triple Sign:

Greetings:
When you need to greet dragons or any other Entity in a dignified and respectful manner, then you can make this gesture. It will inform them that their presence is welcome.

Closure and Banishings:
This method is most commonly used. The magician gives the Triple Sign following an invocation, an important statement, to mark the end of a special stage during a ritual (as an ecclesiastical would do with the sign of the cross) or to conclude a ceremony. When used in this way,

this sign symbolizes that you are taking a significant pause, a conclusion, a banishing of energies or a silent way of saying *so mote it be*.

*
**

PSYCHIC SENSE TRAINING

We now arrive at the heart of your daily training. The following exercises aim to strengthen and increase the power of your most solicited psychic senses during magickal and draconic practices.

If you have always wondered how to gain *magickal powers*, then know that these can only be achieved by special and often, very rigorous training. Indeed (unfortunately for those who imagine that Magick happens without personal effort), I will certainly not be making a great revelation here by telling you that there are no miracle recipes, nor any rituals that can ensure you overnight that you'll be able to perform wonders. There are only three unique ways to achieve this: *practice, practice and practice!*

I believe in you and so the dragons. So please don't be fooled by false prophets! If an author claims that by a simple ritual, which consists, for example, of mixing two handfuls of herbs while chanting by candlelight, and that he confirms you will be able to enjoy unimaginable occult and spiritual powers, the latter is neither a magician nor an occultist. Such a person can only be very misinformed or worse, a charlatan.

While these occult accessories can provide you with excellent support when used wisely, remember that the real Magick is in you! We thought it necessary (PNFYR and I) to warn you about this, because many people blindly believe everything they read, without bothering to validate what feels right or wrong. Take the time to meditate on these words, and you will see, without the shadow of a doubt, how true they are.

To Exercise one's Will

In order to achieve success when practicing Dragon Magick, it is important, first of all, that you can clear your mind and create a void at any time. In this way, you will be able to focus exclusively on what you are doing and nothing else. Imagine for a moment that for some reason, in the midst of a draconic ritual, you came to think what you would eat for dinner! That may sound funny, but it should never happen. This could really harm your Magick rituals and practices.

That explains why the draconic magician knows the importance of exercising his will and to project it where he wishes, but to achieve this, he must first know how to reach a state of mental emptiness. Make no mistake, trying not to think of anything is more difficult than it sounds, but you will eventually get there through this simple exercise.

Sit comfortably, preferably (because lying on your back, eyes closed, chances you'll fall asleep), and light a candle. Stand about one meter from it and take three deep breaths. For now, let your thoughts go, here and there, and pay no attention to them. Then focus on the flame and imagine, to begin with, that just as fire burns oxygen, that flame will consume your thoughts, so that you will not retain any of them in your mind.

Stare at the candle flame and try not to think about anything. Simply stare in silence. As soon as a thought burst into your mind, close your eyes, take a deep breath, then try again.

When you'll be able to keep this state of mental vacuity for ten minutes or so, you'll have mastered this exercise. You will notice after a while that you have come to raise to a higher level of concentration and that your power of visualization will be surprisingly improved.

Visualization

The art of exercising one's psychic eyes to perceive the invisible and see through the mind, *is one of the greatest keys to success in Magick*, if not the basis of every eminent magician. Visualization plays a crucial role in all occult practices, and by this technique, great achievements can be obtained, not to mention that you will have more ease in seeing dragons! This is why the daraco will also take the time to train properly until he masters this technique, because he knows from the outset that all that he will be able to accomplish in Ceremonial and Draconic Magick will principally come to him through his power of visualization.

FIRST DEGREE OF VISUALIZATION

Sit comfortably inside your draconic temple and close your eyes. Clear your mind of all those wandering thoughts that might be assaulting you and focus. Now, imagine a volcano in the distance. See it very imposing, surrounded by trees and vegetation. Small fumes rise just above its crater. A small river flows and winds in front of this volcano. Visualize this whole scene, as if you were looking at a painting. You can add other details as you wish. Hold this image for about ten minutes. Think of nothing but the volcano and the details surrounding it. Once you have managed to focus on this mental imagery without being interrupted by various thoughts, then you will have mastered this exercise and can move on to the next one.

SECOND DEGREE OF VISUALIZATION

This exercise will narrow your focus to encompass more precise details. Close your eyes and imagine your volcano once again, but this time, get closer. You are presently at the foot of the crater, and see big stones here and there on the ground. You notice that there's also soil, tiny rocks and dragon footprints. Pay attention to this area and nothing else. Hold this image for about ten minutes. Think of nothing but what you see before your feet. When you have managed to focus mentally on this image, without being interrupted by stray thoughts, then you will have mastered this exercise and can move on to the next one.

THIRD DEGREE OF VISUALIZATION

This is the last visualization exercise, and also the hardest to master. If you have taken the trouble to practice honestly the previous degrees, you should not encounter to much difficulty with this one. Remember, Draconic Magick is not a race, take all your time and do not perform your daily routine in haste. It won't work.

Close your eyes and return to your volcano. Imagine standing where you previously were, but now instead of seeing rocks and dragon footprints, you curiously notice a strange red rock cut into a triangular shape. Just think of that rock and don't look at anything else. Hold this image in your mind for about ten minutes. Try seeing this triangular stone as clearly as if you were holding it in your hand, as if it really existed. Once you have visualized the stone without being interrupted for ten minutes, try the same thing, but this time, keep your eyes open.

If you can practice this technique in both ways, and capable of seeing any object, as if it were actually there before your eyes, you will then have mastered the visualization exercises.

One of the reasons these exercises were designed to visualize a volcano crater, is because sooner or later, when you'll want to meet the Fire dragons, you will need to mentally travel there, directly in their realm, and a volcano is a place of choice to find the fiery Element. By then, you shouldn't experience any trouble visualizing it when comes the time to converse with the red dragons; you will have travelled there every day! You will have accomplished two

things at once. In addition, you can also pursue your training with the other Elements, for example, by travelling to
the outskirts of a lake for the Water Element, etc.

Psychic Hearing

The psychic ear is necessary if you want to capture the
sounds and understand dragon as well as dialogs from all
the Spirits inhabiting the Draconic Zone and other planes
of existence. In other words, to be able to truly hear dragons when they speak to you (or any other Spirit), as if you
were talking to a human being, you must practice hearing
what your physical hearing cannot. To do this, you'll start
by imagining simple, specific sounds. This exercise will require the use of a small bell, the one you will use during
the Opening and Closing Rites.

Sit comfortably in your draconic temple. Close your
eyes and ring your bell a few times while listening carefully. Remember the particularities of this soft and sharp
sound. Now imagine you are ringing the bell again, without actually doing so. Hear the bell ring again and again in
your mind, continuously for about ten minutes. Do not visualize the bell; you only have to hear it. If at any time you
find it difficult to reproduce the sound of your bell, ring it
once or twice to remind you of the sound it produces, and
then continue to hear the chime.

When you easily imagine the sound of your bell, try
something new, like a drop of water, a piano note or a vio-
lin string, a clock ticking or hands clapping, etc.

The final stage of this psychic ear training will consist in hearing voices, close to you as much as if they came from afar, at a very long distance, proceeding in the same way. This exercise will have achieved its goal by the time you are able to recreate any sound, without difficulty.

PSYCHIC TOUCH

Psychic touch means being able to feel phenomena and sensations belonging to the world of dragons and invisible planes in an almost physical way. Moreover, when this sense is well trained, it will emphasize your power of intuition by what is called psychometry. This technique will give you the opportunity to feel the forces manifested on the etheric plane, and you will thus be endowed with the ability to perceive the past, present or future just by touching everything, any object through the psychic touch. You'll even be able to feel the breath of dragons.

To get started, go ahead with simple, easy-to-feel sensations like heat, coldness, dampness, heaviness, etc. For example, imagine the feeling of an ice cube sitting in the palm of your hand. To make it easier, you can hold, per instance, a real cube in your right hand for a few seconds. Then remove it, close your eyes and try to feel the same tactile sensation but in your left hand, without ever visualizing the ice cube. The idea of feeling the real object at first is to stimulate your sense of touch. Then you could move on and try with heat. For this, you can light a candle and put your hands just above it. Then remove them, close your eyes and recreate the same warm feeling.

Once you have acquired the ability to experience any type of physical sensation, without visualizing it, for a period of five to ten minutes, you will have mastered the exercise.

Just as you practiced exercises for the last two psychic senses, if you want to perfect your draconic training and push your abilities to the maximum, then know that you can use the same technique for the sense of taste and smell, imagining flavors and their smells. That way all your magician senses will become powerful and well balanced.

*
**

MEDITATING AND CONVERSING WITH DRAGONS

This is the exercise pertaining to the seventh statement of the Draconic Code: *to meditate and converse*. This method is by far the one you will use the most to communicate with dragons. As they are able to feel the energies you project toward them, not only will you be able to create a powerful bond with them and the Draconic Force, but by opening your mind in this state of mental passivity, you'll be capable to receive the many messages they will communicate you.

Having completed their magickal training, it will be easy for you to converse with the draconic Beings, for you will have skillfully developed all your psychic senses. In this way, dragons will reveal numerous things to you. You will receive fantastic visions about things past, present or future. You will be able to distinguish the colorful forms of energy and images, places and landscapes that may be unknown, see the inhabitants of the subtle worlds and many other sensations that will be very real.

Meditation will elevate your consciousness to the necessary level so that your familiar dragons, or any other draconic Beings, may converse with you. True, it is quite possible in the beginning, when you'll get your very first results, to doubt your senses or, for some reason, to feel that what you saw was just the product of your imagination. Know your visions and conversations; they will be authentic, just like dragons are...

THE TECHNIQUE

Guided draconic meditation is very similar to the Major Rite of the first degree of the *Initiatory Passage of the Draconia*. Sit comfortably and relax your whole body. You can light candles if desired, and burn incense, or even play some relaxing, soft and pleasant music, but not too rhythmic.

Now, close your eyes and imagine you are walking, under a beautiful starry night of a full moon, on a path marked by small stones from which emanates a faint white glow. Walk slowly, until you finally approach the side of a mountain where you distinguish the features of a very large cave. Its entrance is curiously shaped like a dragon's mouth. Entering this cave, you continue your way down on a slowly sloping path, as the presence of dragons is becoming stronger and stronger. Keep traveling deeper and deeper.

You now realize you're draped in a red and dazzling aura. This warm brightness is omnipresent; this is the Draconic Force. As you continue your descent, finally, right in front of you, at the end of a long passageway, stands a huge silver door. You push it gently with your hand and walk inside. As you enter, you find yourself in a huge circular room. At the same exact moment, a strong and intense pulsating light momentarily blinds you and envelops your entire body. You are now in the heart of Draconia.

In the center of the room stands a beautiful ruby-colored soft carpet with silver edges. The presence of dragons is felt more than ever, they are very close to you. You decide to take place in the center of the carpet and sit down. Now close your eyes and let go...

This is how works the technique of draconic meditation and conversation. Once you sit on the ruby silver carpet and close your eyes, think no more and allow the course of meditation do the rest. From this point, I can't tell you exactly what will happen next, because only you will be able to see what will be the outcome of this exercise, and what kind messages dragons might want to reveal you, either by form of speech or mental imagery.

When you're done, mentally walk back and return to the cave exit, then open your eyes. Write down everything you have seen and heard in your diary so as not to forget anything about this experience, which will undoubtedly be exceptional.

HARNESSING DRACONIC POWER

I N addition to experiencing all around you, tangibly, manifestations of the mighty Draconic Force, you must know how to properly accumulate it, so you'll be able to use it according to your will, during your magickal workings. Among other practical uses, you will be able to compress it into a ball of sparkling energy (which even a profane would be able to see with his flesh eyes, if you have obtained enough mastery), compacted to such an extent that it will be easy to charge any place with a vibrating aura of a specific nature, as well as charging your magickal tools and accessories, like talismans and other objects. You'll have the means to act directly on the elemental forces of the Universe and even the possibility to give birth to artificial psychic entities, which will have a certain level of consciousness and autonomy, to name but a few examples.

When this technique is properly used along with the power of visualization, be certain that it will become possible for you to accomplish unimaginable things to common people, which some might even describe as... miracles.

STEP ONE: THE RESPIRATORY ORGAN

The following is the preliminary technique used to accumulate the Draconic Force; you're going to compress it through conscious skin breathing. Start by taking a position that will not cause any discomfort or aches. Then close your eyes, if it's easier to practice visualization this way, otherwise you can keep them open. Now, imagine your body is like a sponge being plunged into the water. Breathe deeply. Visualize the air penetrating your body not only via your nostrils or mouth, but also through all the pores of your skin; by the head, back, arms, hands, torso, legs, feet, etc., identical to our previous sponge. Your whole body must become one respiratory organ. Then exhale the accumulated air the same way.

Once you are able to master this simple technique, it will be easy for you to use it for various purposes, including impregnating yourself with a quality when inhaling as well as dissolving a negative quality when exhaling, seeing it leave your body.

STEP TWO: ACCUMULATION BY BREATHING

Now, we need to take the breathing exercise a step further so that you can effectively accumulate the Draconic Force. Get back to your usual position and make sure your body is relaxed. Then visualize being in the center of the Universe. In front of you is a magnificent golden-red, sparkling, pulsating sphere. This sphere of energy is the raw Draconic Force. When you are able to visualize it as clearly as if you would with your physical eyes, you can continue the exercise. Next, inhale this energy deeply through all the pores of your skin. Imagine as you breathe, that a ray of light is transferred from the sphere, directly into you, through your whole body. Your body sucks in and concentrate this powerful energy inside. It becomes a receptacle accumulating light.

When exhaling, nothing should come out of your body. The Draconic Force will remain permanently kept inside. Breathe in again and keep accumulating this light by charging it with a specific quality, seeing it penetrate you from everywhere, until you feel this energy is compressed to such a degree that you can no longer take it, like a balloon too swollen that is about to burst.

At this point, know that you will have properly accumulated enough Draconic Force to use it for magickal purposes. Now you just need to decide how you wish to transfer this light-energy, as shown in step three.

STEP THREE: IMPREGNATION AND TRANSFER

There are several ways to use the Draconic Force in order to transfer and charge one's surroundings. The way you plan to use it will determinate how to transfer this powerful energy currently compressed into your body. There are two basic techniques for achieving this, direct and indirect; either through the solar plexus and exhalation, or through the hands and fingertips. We're going to take a closer look at these two techniques.

I.— EXPULSION THROUGH THE SOLAR PLEXUS

Transferring the Draconic Force through the solar plexus is the most appropriate method for any type of charge of an indirect nature. We understand by "indirect" everything that does not concern an immediate action on a particular person or object, but rather a charge of a general nature such as the impregnation of a place, where the effects will be felt by all beings (visible and invisible) in the vicinity. The transfer will be done pretty much the same way as before, as you did earlier to accumulate the Draconic Force, but in reverse.

Breathe in deeply and then breathe out slowly. When you exhale, visualize the accumulated and highly compressed Draconic Force, expelling itself through your solar plexus, like a jet of light or vapor escaping from your body to imbue the room or the place where you are at that moment. Have the certainty that the area will vibrate the projected quality. Inhale again, without visualizing anything, then exhale and visualize once more the energy leaving your body, bit by bit, charging the atmosphere, and so on. You should normally use as many exhalations to transfer this Force from your body as there have been inhalations to accumulate it in you. When your body is empty, the Draconic Force fully transferred, the exercise will be completed and will have reached its goal.

*
**

II.— EXPULSION THROUGH HANDS OR FINGERS

Transferring the Draconic Force through the hands or fingers is a direct induction method. This means the charge will pass directly from one subject to another, from the daraco to a person, an object, etc.

You have two choices to achieve this. You can, by applying your hands, transfer the light-charge onto the subject by exhaling as explained above. Instead of passing through the solar plexus, it will go through the hands. This method is very effective for healing the body or diseased limbs as well as charging magickal tools and wands, as well as talismanic objects. You will use as many exhalations to transfer the Draconic Force as there have been inspirations to accumulate it in you.

The other method, just as effective, is to expel and impregnate the energy in a single movement, as if you were projecting a lightning bolt from your fingertips. To achieve this, you must first compress the Draconic Force, which is in your entire body, into one of your hands. When you are able to see all this compressed power in a tiny radiating spark on the tips of your fingers, shoot in the desired direction towards the subject who will receive this magickal charge. This technique is often used to dissolve and kill artificial elementals, including thought forms and Elementaries created by the mage.

REMARKS

Depending on your goals, you will have charged this light with a quality when breathing in. If, for example, you wanted to charge a place with a protective shield, by breathing in this pure energy, you would merely need to think very strongly about the desired protection. In the same way, you can induce healing qualities, and then transfer that Draconic Force onto the afflicted person, etc.

Conscious pore breathing also works the same way, by its application and operation, in order to accumulate and control the Cosmic and Primary elemental Forces, Air, Water, Fire, Earth and Akâsha. You will therefore use this technique for this purpose.

If you're into spellcasting, you can charge magickal objects with these techniques; anything like amulets, stones, potions, even statuettes placed at specific spots in your home to provide different effects and goals, etc.

The possibilities here are virtually *endless*. Harnessing dragon power is one of the true secrets of occultism. Remember, however, that the power conferred by this high magickal practice should be used only for good, justice, and to help others or oneself.

CHARGING AND CONSECRATING DRACONIC TOOLS

O NCE you have crafted your basic draconic tools, it will be time to charge them with their respective Element, one at a time, so that they become dedicated to the Works of Draconia and for that purpose only. These magickal tools will be of no use to you except for Dragon Magick and other practices of High Magick.

Even if you got all your tools ready to be used, I strongly recommend you do not consecrate them all at the same time, because there would be just too much a blend of elemental energies involved. Additionally, if you perform theses ritual with heart and meticulousness, you might become too exhausted after only one or two reiterations.

For example, you could charge one tool per day. There's no point hurrying. For reasons you may understand later, it is better to take a whole week to charge and consecrate your draconic instruments than to repeat over and over the same tiring ceremony.

EARTH PENTACLE CONSECRATION RITUAL

Perform the Draconic Cross ritual.

Perform the Opening Ritual.

Facing North, hold your elemental Pentacle in your right hand. Then say in a solemn and humble tone:

O Thou, Eternal, Mother and Father of all things, Thou who dost clothe Thyself with the forces of nature and of the Universe, I beseech Thou Holy presence to grant me strength and inner vision as I search for inner Wisdom within Thy hidden Light.

I humbly request, as a disciple of Thy Cosmic Laws, that Thou mayest cause Thy Draconic King GRAËL to guide me on my holy journey on the Universal paths of Draconia, during my personal, magickal and spiritual quest.

May the ruler of the Earth, the powerful GRAËL, by the permission of the Eternal One, increase and strengthen the secret forces and virtues of this Pentacle so that I may use it to perform those magickal rituals and practices for which it has been fashioned. It is to this end that I now perform this rite of consecration in the presence of the Divine and Draconic Force.

Replace the Pentacle on the altar and trace over an Earth Invoking Pentagram, in the same way as explained for the Draconic Cross ritual. Visualize it in a very bright green. Continue:

By the three Great Names of the One borne upon the glorious banners of the North; MOR-DIAL-HKTGA (Moh-ar-Dee-ah-leh-Heh-keh-teh-gah), **I summon Thee to be here and now, oh Thou Great Draconic King of the North, GRAËL, and Thou, oh Great King of the Northern Quarter, IKZHIKAL** (Ee-keh-zod-heh-kal). **Increase the effect of this ritual whose purpose is to consecrate this Draconic instrument of Magick. Give it power now to be more than capable in all works of Earth so that by it I may find a strong defense and powerful weapon to direct the Spirits of this Elements, according to my will, as is dictated by the One whom naught but silence can express.**

Now, take a comfortable position, either standing or siting, and hold the Pentacle at the chest level. Close your eyes and visualize being in the center of the Universe. In front of you is a beautiful green, radiant and pulsating sphere. This highly charged energetic sphere is the purest representation of the Cosmic Element of Earth, as if a vast elemental ocean was compressed therein. Now, inhale this energy deeply through all the pores of your skin, using the technique of conscious breathing. Visualize, as you breathe in, that the Element is transferred from the elemental sphere, directly into you, through your entire body.

While breathing out, nothing is expelled; the accumulated energy permanently remains in you. Continue accumulating the Earth Element in this fashion until you feel it compressed in your body to such a degree that you can no longer hold any more.

Finally, focus your attention on the Pentacle and begin transferring the Element of Earth by direct induction. Expel all elemental energy accumulated through your hands. With each exhalation, see the energy impregnating the tool, which will shine brighter and brighter with a green and extremely vivid aura.

Conclude the consecration ritual with the Draconic Cross. This second time, instead of tracing four Banishing Pentagrams of the Earth, you will replace them with four Invoking Pentagrams of the same Element, which will be traced with your newly charged Pentacle.

Seal your Magick temple by performing the Closing Ritual. When finished, wrap your Pentacle in a green, brown or white silk or cotton fabric. Once consecrated, make sure no one touches your draconic tool.

AIR DAGGER CONSECRATION RITUAL

Perform the Draconic Cross ritual.

Perform the Opening Ritual.

Facing East, hold your elemental Dagger in your right hand. Then say in a solemn and humble tone:

O Thou, Eternal, Mother and Father of all things, Thou who dost clothe Thyself with the forces of nature and of the Universe, I beseech Thou Holy presence to grant me strength and inner vision as I search for inner Wisdom within Thy hidden Light.

I humbly request, as a disciple of Thy Cosmic Laws, that Thou mayest cause Thy Draconic King SAIRYS to guide me on my holy journey on the Universal paths of Draconia, during my personal, magickal and spiritual quest.

May the ruler of AIR, the powerful SAIRYS, by the permission of the Eternal One, increase and strengthen the secret forces and virtues of this Dagger so that I may use it to perform those magickal rituals and practices for which it has been fashioned. It is to this end that I now perform this rite of consecration in the presence of the Divine and of the Draconic Force.

Replace the Dagger on the altar and trace over an Air Invoking Pentagram. Visualize it in a very bright yellow. Continue:

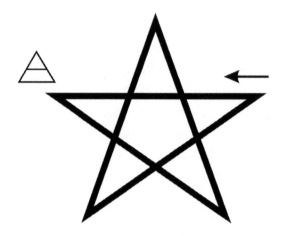

By the three Great Names of the One borne upon the glorious banners of the East; ORO-IBAH-AOZPI (Oh-roh-Eh-bah-Ah-oh-zod-peh), **I summon Thee to be here and now, oh Thou Great Draconic King of the East, SAIRYS, and Thou, oh Great King of the Eastern Quarter, BATAIVAH** (Bah-tah-eh-vah-heh). **Increase the effect of this ritual whose purpose is to consecrate this Draconic instrument of Magick. Give it power now to be more than capable in all works of Air so that by it I may find a strong defense and powerful weapon to direct the Spirits of this Elements, according to my will, as is dictated by the One whom naught but silence can express.**

Now, take a comfortable position, either standing or siting, and hold the Dagger, point up, at chest level. Close your eyes and visualize being in the center of the Universe. In front of you is a beautiful yellow, radiant and pulsating sphere. This highly charged energetic sphere is the purest representation of the Cosmic Element of Air, as if a vast elemental ocean was compressed therein. Now, inhale this energy deeply through all the pores of your skin, using the technique of conscious breathing. Imagine as you breathe in, that the Element is transferred from the elemental sphere, directly into you, through your entire body.

While breathing out, nothing is expelled; the accumulated energy permanently remains in you. Continue accumulating the Air Element this fashion until you feel it compressed in your body to such a degree that you can no longer hold any more.

Finally, focus your attention on the Dagger and begin to transfer the Air Element by direct induction. Expel all elemental energy accumulated through your hands. With each exhalation, see the energy impregnating the tool, which will shine brighter and brighter with a yellow and extremely bright aura.

Conclude the consecration ritual with the Draconic Cross. This second time, instead of tracing four Banishing Pentagrams of the Earth, you will replace them with four Air Invoking Pentagrams, traced with your newly charged Dagger.

Seal your sanctuary by performing the Closing Ritual. Wrap your Dagger in a yellow or white silk or cotton fabric. Once consecrated, make sure no one touches your draconic tool.

Water Cup Consecration Ritual

Perform the Draconic Cross ritual.

Perform the Opening Ritual.

Facing West, hold your elemental Cup in your right hand. Then say in a solemn and humble tone:

O Thou, Eternal, Mother and Father of all things, Thou who dost clothe Thyself with the forces of nature and of the Universe, I beseech Thou Holy presence to grant me strength and inner vision as I search for inner Wisdom within Thy hidden Light.

I humbly request, as a disciple of Thy Cosmic Laws, that Thou mayest cause Thy Draconic King NAËLYAN to guide me on my holy journey on the Universal paths of Draconia, during my personal, magickal and spiritual quest.

May the ruler of Water, the powerful NAËLYAN, by the permission of the Eternal One, increase and strengthen the secret forces and virtues of this Chalice so that I may use it to perform those magickal rituals and practices for which it has been fashioned. It is to this end that I now perform this rite of consecration in the presence of the Divine and of the Draconic Force.

Replace the Cup on the altar and trace over a Water Invoking Pentagram. Visualize it in a very bright blue. Continue:

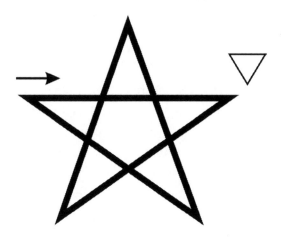

By the three Great Names of the One borne upon the glorious banners of the West; MPH-ARSL-GAIOL (Em-peh-heh-Ar-ess-el-Gah-eh-oh-leh), I summon Thee to be here and now, oh Thou Great Draconic King of the West, NAËLYAN, and Thou, oh Great King of the Western Quarter, RAAGIOSL (Rah-ah-geh-oh-sel). Increase the effect of this ritual whose purpose is to consecrate this Draconic instrument of Magick. Give it power now to be more than capable in all works of Water so that by it I may find a strong defense and powerful weapon to direct the Spirits of this Elements, according to my will, as is dictated by the One whom naught but silence can express.

Now, take a comfortable position, either standing or siting, and hold the Cup at the chest level. Close your eyes and visualize being in the center of the Universe. In front of you is a beautiful blue, radiant and pulsating sphere. This highly charged energetic sphere is the purest representation of the Cosmic Element of Water, as if a vast elemental ocean was compressed therein. Now, inhale this energy deeply through all the pores of your skin, using the technique of conscious breathing. Visualize as you breathe in, that the Element is transferred from the elemental sphere, directly into you, through your entire body.

While breathing out, nothing is expelled; the accumulated energy permanently remains in you. Continue accumulating the Water Element this fashion until you feel it compressed in your body to such a degree that you can no longer hold any more.

Finally, focus your attention on the Cup and begin to transfer the Element of Water by direct induction. Expel all elemental energy accumulated through your hands. With each exhalation, see the energy impregnating the tool, which will shine brighter and brighter with a blue and extremely bright aura.

Conclude the consecration ritual with the Draconic Cross. This second time, instead of tracing four Banishing Pentagrams of the Earth, you will replace them with four Water Invoking Pentagrams, traced with your newly charged Cup.

Seal your sanctuary by performing the Closing Ritual. Wrap your Cup in a blue or white silk or cotton fabric. Once consecrated, make sure no one touches your draconic tool.

FIRE WAND CONSECRATION RITUAL

Perform the Draconic Cross ritual.

Perform the Opening Ritual.

Facing South, hold your elemental Wand in your right hand. Then say in a solemn and humble tone:

O Thou, Eternal, Mother and Father of all things, Thou who dost clothe Thyself with the forces of nature and of the Universe, I beseech Thou Holy presence to grant me strength and inner vision as I search for inner Wisdom within Thy hidden Light.

I humbly request, as a disciple of Thy Cosmic Laws, that Thou mayest cause Thy Draconic King FAFNYR to guide me on my holy journey on the Universal paths of Draconia, during my personal, magickal and spiritual quest.

May the ruler of Fire, the powerful FAFNYR, by the permission of the Eternal One, increase and strengthen the secret forces and virtues of this Wand so that I may use it to perform those magickal rituals and practices for which it has been fashioned. It is to this end that I now perform this rite of consecration in the presence of the Divine and of the Draconic Force.

Replace the Wand on the altar and trace over a Fire Invoking Pentagram. Visualize it in a very bright red. Continue:

By the three Great Names of the One borne upon the glorious banners of the South; OIP-TEAA-PDOKE (Oh-ee-peh-Teh-ah-ah-Peh-doh-keh), **I summon Thee to be here and now, oh Thou Great Draconic King of the South, FAFNYR, and Thou, oh Great King of the Southern Quarter, EDLPRNAA** (Eh-del-par-nah-ah). **Increase the effect of this ritual whose purpose is to consecrate this Draconic instrument of Magick. Give it power now to be more than capable in all works of Fire so that by it I may find a strong defense and powerful weapon to direct the Spirits of this Elements, according to my will, as is dictated by the One whom naught but silence can express.**

Now, take a comfortable position, either standing or siting, and hold the Wand at the chest level, pointing up. Close your eyes and visualize being in the center of the Universe. In front of you is a beautiful red, radiant and pulsating sphere. This highly charged energetic sphere is the purest representation of the Cosmic Element of Fire, as if a vast elemental ocean was compressed therein. Now, inhale this energy deeply through all the pores of your skin, using the technique of conscious breathing. Imagine as you breathe in, that the Element is transferred from the elemental sphere, directly into you, through your entire body.

While breathing out, nothing is expelled; the accumulated energy permanently remains in you. Continue accumulating the Fire Element this fashion until you feel it compressed in your body to such a degree that you can no longer hold any more.

Finally, focus your attention on the Wand and begin to transfer the Element of Fire by direct induction. Expel all elemental energy accumulated through your hands. With each exhalation, see the energy impregnating the tool, which will shine brighter and brighter with a red and extremely vivid aura.

Conclude the consecration ritual with the Draconic Cross. This second time, instead of tracing four Banishing Pentagrams of the Earth, you will replace them with four Fire Invoking Pentagrams, traced with your newly charged Wand.

Seal your sanctuary by performing the Closing Ritual. Wrap your Wand in a red or white silk or cotton fabric. Once consecrated, make sure no one touches your draconic tool.

THE DRACONIC SCRIPT

I N Draconic Magick there is a form of written language called the Dragon Script. These symbols, corresponding to the letters of our alphabet, have been used for a long time by the daracos for all their ritual writing needs.

A	B	C,K	D	E	F

G	H	I,J	L	M	N

O,Q	P	R	S	T	U,V

W	X	Y	Z	*End of sentence*

You can do several things: whether making talismans, talismanic images, writing power names on your runes or transcribing complete ceremonies into your grimoire. In short, draconic creatures will appreciate you use their script whenever possible, if you are authorized to do so.

CODA DRACONIS

Tail of the Dragon

# Major Draconic Rites

T HE third part of this book, dedicated to the pres-
tigious Draconia, contains the most important
magickal and ceremonial practices of the daraco.
These rituals are called the Major Rites because they are
the most frequently performed. These are the means by
which you'll most often express the Draconic Teachings.

There are indeed many other practices closely related
to Dragon Magick. Some of these rituals are as elaborate
and authentic as the ones you are about to discover. They
shall be revealed to you at another time, when I'll be allowed to do so. In the meantime, just stay aware, as you
might discover along your journey other "draconic rituals", which sometimes turn out to be nothing more than
mere derivatives of the Major Rites. Study them carefully
to authenticate them and don't hesitate to ask one of your
familiar dragons for assistance in finding out where they
came from and obtaining approval for their implementa-
tion.

In any case, the eleven rituals that follows, considering
that the Rite of Opening and Closing are in reality only a
single rite divided into two distinct parts, are the most im-

portant to ponder for the moment in the context of your magickal training, as a dignitary of the Dragon Science.

Before turning to practice, if I may suggest this final recommendation; I would advise to always stay on the path of wisdom and remain patient at all times! Start by reading the rituals thoroughly to understand their meaning and impact on the subtle planes. Write notes, if necessary, copy them in full in your grimoire and try to memorize them. Consistency and perseverance will greatly reward all your efforts.

Take the trouble to make things right, as you should. After all, shouldn't we say that what deserves to be done must be done well? Exclusively in this way will you be able to reach the pinnacle of your aspirations and recognize not only that Draconic Magick is unique, extremely satisfying, but also very powerful!

# THE DRACONIC CROSS RITUAL

H ERE is a ritual of Ceremonial Magick from the High Draconia. It is very similar to the Lesser Banishing Ritual of the Pentagram (LBRP). Its main function is to connect you directly to the divine source, the Cosmic Light, which governs everything that exists, including dragons, and to let this beneficent energy flow through your body and diffuse it in all directions. You will be able to effectively banish from your immediate surroundings all hostile and unwanted influences with the support and power of the four Draconic Kings. In other words, this ritual is an ideal preliminary to purify your magickal temple before any Draconic Magick or as a protection rite, not to mention the fact that *it creates an excellent Magick circle by itself.*

Moreover, no tools are needed to perform this ritual, except your draconic dagger or sword, if desired, without forgetting your power of visualization, nothing more. If you do not have your ceremonial tools at that moment, it's not dramatic, as nothing should prevent you from practicing today. To do this, simply use the index finger of your right hand. You can also burn a white candle, but this is not mandatory.

By repeating this ritual on a daily basis, preferably once a day, you will be able to expand your aura (or vibratory field), generate and control draconic and spiritual energies, thereby increasing your perception through your psychic senses, and directly connecting you to the strength of dragons. It is probably impossible or unimaginable for you at this time to measure all the benefits of such a magickal practice; what awaits you may surprise you even more. Believe my experience, there are many benefits in performing this ritual meticulously. That said, it is possible at first glance that you find the ritual a little complex and even a bit long. Worry not. After a few serious rehearsals, you'll find out it's possible to memorize it by heart and perform in less than ten minutes, even if you slowly take your time.

Final note: if you do not have sufficient space nor an entirely dedicated room to practice Magick, you can always trace a small circle around you and simply pivot on your axis in order to face the different Watchtowers. A little trick to help you remember the names to pronounce; you could, for example, just stick on the walls of your room, little cards with the names on them so you can read them, if needed.

VIBRATING MAGICKAL NAMES

In Ceremonial Magick, the vibrating of names is constantly used. And for good reason, this process "charges" and empowers any form of ritual verbalization. The goal is to visualize oneself in the center of the Universe and deeply breathe in the magickal name, feeling the energy coming by inhalation and visualization, through the entire body, down to the lower limbs. Then, *for the entire duration of the expiration*, the name will rise up the length of the body and be projected outside of the outer limits of the Universe, in a clash of power and resonance, like a gigantic thunder. Use this technique for the Draconic Cross as well as for all other rituals, whatever they may be, and whenever it is specified to *vibrate* a magickal name.

*
**

PART ONE: THE DRACONIC CROSS

Trace a magick circle mentally, with your dagger, ceremonial sword or with the index finger of your dominant hand. Afterwards, stand in the center, facing East. Visualize your body growing taller and larger. Continue expanding like this, rising above your home, your city, until the Earth becomes a tiny sphere, very far below you. You go beyond the stars, planets, galaxies... Continue your ascent until you find yourself in the very center of the Universe. Remember, however, that your feet must remain firmly anchored to the ground at all times. You are perpetually connected and deeply rooted to the Earth.

Now, look over your head; see a tiny speck of light. Pursue your growth to get closer, until this sphere of light becomes about the size of a ball. Then take a few moments to contemplate it. This light is of extreme brilliance, white and pulsating, as radiant as thousands of suns combined in one; it is the Primordial Divine Source. Now point your dagger (sword or index finger) towards it and draw down a shaft of light to your forehead. This last step is most important because it directly connects your Higher Self to the Divine. The words in parentheses indicate the pronunciation.

Vibrate: **ZAH** (Zod-ah)

Now, still with your dagger (or finger), draw the light beam by pointing the blade down, at the lower abdomen. Feel this column of pure light passing through your body, to the very edge of the Universe, far below you.

Vibrate: **ONDOH** (Oh-en-doh)

Then raise your dagger up along your torso up to your throat. Now touch your right shoulder, visualizing that the light follows this same movement to go to the fastest reaches of the Universe, to your right.

Vibrate: **MIH** (Mee-heh)

Similarly, slowly touch your left shoulder, bringing the beam of light to that side too.

Vibrate: **BUZD** (Boo-zod-deh)

Then join hands, as you would if they were joined for

praying. Now view in the center of your chest a beautiful and soft golden sphere extremely bright.

Vibrate: **PAID** (Pah-ee-deh) **STELOI** (Steh-loh-eh)

Taking a few seconds to see what you have just accomplished; you realize that you're at the center of a Universal Cross of Divine Light that touches all the furthest reaches of the Cosmos.

The words you just vibrated correspond respectively to the following sentence: *"Here within is the kingdom, and the power, and the glory, forever. So mote it be."* Take time to understand the full meaning and impact of your words when you pronounce them, for you are addressing yourself directly to the Universal Divine Power.

PART TWO: THE FORMULATION OF THE PENTAGRAMS

Walk to the boundaries of your circle, always facing East. Using your sword, dagger or index finger, trace a Banishing Pentagram of Earth in the air in front of you. Begin at the lower left tip, as shown in the following figure.

To help you draw the Pentagram of the right size, use your body as a guide. Start at your left hip and trace the first side up to your forehead. From there, go down to your right hip. Now go up to the left shoulder, then to your right shoulder, and finally complete the Pentagram by returning to your starting point, at the left hip. Visualize as you draw the Pentagram, a flame gushing from the tip of your dagger (sword or index finger), such as the fire of a welding torch. This light shall be visualized in flames of a very bright electric blue.

Banishing Pentagram of Earth

Now, you will do the God Form called the *Sign of the Enterer*. You will bring your hands to either side of your head, pointing the blade and fingers forward, while taking a deep breath. Breathe the energy into your body. When you exhale, make one step forward with your left foot. At the same time, thrust your hands at the center of the pentagram with force, while vibrating:

ORO-IBAH-AOZPI (Oh-roh-Eh-bah-Ah-oh-zod-peh)

Feel the energy of this Divine name travelling out of your body, passing through your hands, into the precise center of the Pentagram. Return to your previous position and join your feet again, but keep your sword (dagger or index finger) still pointing at the center of the Pentagram. Then, draw a line of light in the air, walking along the outskirts of your circle, to the South. Visualize this line of a bright white. The latter will connect all your Pentagrams together. Facing the South, draw another Banishing Pentagram of Earth as you just did. Then again, make the Sign of the Enterer while vibrating:

OIP-TEAA-PDOKE
(Oh-ee-peh-Teh-ah-ah-Peh-doh-keh)

Carry the line of white light to the West. Trace a third Pentagram there. Make the Sign of the Enterer while vibrating:

MPH-ARSL-GAIOL
(Em-peh-heh-Ar-ess-el-Gah-eh-oh-leh)

Now go to the North carrying the line. Facing North, trace the last Pentagram. Make the Sign of the Enterer and vibrate:

MOR-DIAL-HKTGA
(Moh-ar-Dee-ah-leh-Heh-keh-teh-gah)

Return to your starting point in the East, completing this circle of light. Then return to your initial position in the center of the magickal circle and face East.

Line of Light connecting the Pentagrams

You are now circled by four electric blue Pentagrams. These are sealed by the four great divine names; the whole being connected by a line made of pure white light. Now turn your attention to this line. See it thicken up and down, making a column or a sphere that extends to the furthest reaches of the Universe.

PART THREE: THE EVOCATION OF THE DRACONIC KINGS

Stretch your arms to the sides, your body forming a cross. The blade of your magickal instrument should point upwards. Now, visualize that you are a white, shining cross in the center of the Universe. Admire in front of you a large and majestic dragon standing on a hill. He has yellow scales with reflections of the purest mauve. Powerful winds are blowing towards you, coming from behind this draconic King who holds a dagger in his paw. Feel those winds then say:

Before me stands SAIRYS (vibrate the name).

Now visualize a great and noble dragon behind you in the West. His scales are of a silvery blue, illuminated with orange highlights. He holds a crystal chalice in one of his paws. Waterfalls surround this draconic King. Feel the humidity in the air and hear the clash of water. Then say:

Behind me stands NAËLYAN (vibrate the name).

On your right, visualize a powerful and imposing dragon with red scales shining with green reflections. This draconic King holds a blazing sword. Feel the heat from the South. Say:

To my right stands FAFNYR (vibrate the name).

To your left, visualize a large dragon standing securely on fertile land. His scales are in shades of green and brown. This draconic King holds a twig of wheat in his mouth. Feel the stability of the Earth and say:

To my left stands GRAËL (vibrate the name).

Open outwards with your left foot, spreading your legs apart and stretch your arms on either side. You are now forming a human star. Visualize that your body is highlighted by an electric blue Pentagram. Pronounce:

For about me flames the Draconic Pentagram...

Visualize a gleaming, golden Hexagram, the six-pointed star, shining and radiating at your solar plexus, and conclude:

...and within me shines the Six-Ray Star.

Part Four: The Draconic Cross

Repeat the first part of this ritual: the Draconic Cross. The ritual is now complete.

∗

SUMMARY OF THE DRACONIC CROSS RITUAL

To help you memorize this ritual, here is a summary without the explanations pertaining to visualization.

- *Part One: The Draconic Cross*

  Touch your forehead and vibrate: **ZAH**
  Point down and vibrate: **ONDOH**
  Touch your right shoulder and vibrate: **MIH**
  Touch your left shoulder and vibrate: **BUZD**
  Then join hands and vibrate: **PAID, STELOI**

- *Part Two: The Formulation of the Pentagrams*

  Trace the Pentagram in the East. Vibrate:
  ORO-IBAH-AOZPI
  Trace the Pentagram in the South. Vibrate:
  OIP-TEAA-PDOKE
  Trace the Pentagram in the West. Vibrate:
  MPH-ARSL-GAIOL
  Trace the Pentagram in the North. Vibrate:
  MOR-DIAL-HKTGA

- *Part Three: The Evocation of the Draconic Kings*

  Open your arms, forming a cross, and say:
  Before me stands SAIRYS
  Behind me stands NAËLYAN
  To my right stands FAFNYR

To my left stands GRAËL
For about me flames the Draconic Pentagram,
And within me shines the Six-rayed Star.

- *Part Four: The Draconic Cross*

  Touch your forehead and vibrate: **ZAH**
  Point down and vibrate: **ONDOH**
  Touch your right shoulder and vibrate: **MIH**
  Touch your left shoulder and vibrate: **BUZD**
  Then join hands and vibrate: **PAID, STELOI**

THE DRACONIC HEXAGRAM RITUAL

T HE Hexagram Ritual is the "sister" rite of the
Draconic Cross. The two are similar on several levels, and their functions are virtually identical. One
almost never goes without the other; they are complementary. The difference between these two rituals, apart from
the fact that one makes use of the Pentagram and the other
of the Hexagram, lies in their banishing actions.

The Hexagram Ritual has the effect of banning planetary influences and high or positive Entities from your immediate surroundings, unlike the Draconic Cross, which
among other uses, banishes all astral and negative influences. This explains why these two rituals complement
each other perfectly.

You are probably right to ask yourself what good is
chasing Entities or positive influences from your magickal
temple, if they are... beneficial! The reason is simple. When
performing rituals, whether Ceremonial or Draconic
Magick, the last thing you want to see is an outside influence interfering with your work, whatever they may be.

So, imagine for a moment you're practicing a ritual and that some positive Entities, being nearby, are jumping in to help you out, even if it's only for your own good. You would lose control of the ritual at that very moment, without ever being aware.

This explains why you should always perform this ritual, immediately after the Draconic Cross, in order to clean and banish all that is unwelcomed in your Temple, being evil or good. Afterwards, just as you do during the Opening Rite, the only presences in your Temple will be those invited and evoked by you.

ABOUT THE HEXAGRAMS

You'll notice that the Hexagrams used in the ritual are not exactly like the ones we're used to see traditionally. Instead of drawing four different Hexagrams, namely, one for each Element, all consisting of a pair of triangles, here you will employ the Unicursal Hexagram.

The variation that exists in these symbols only affects this ritual. They represent the banishment of planetary influences. Thus, it is possible to use only one type of Hexagram; the Unicursal. You can achieve the same effects by starting from the top to bottom, on the right (see the following figure). This position implies the banishment of Saturnian forces, which encompass all other planetary influences, when referring to the position of the Sephirah Binah (Saturn) in the Kabbalistic Tree of Life.

*
**

Part One: The formulation of the Hexagrams

Head to the boundaries of your circle, always facing East (or pivot on yourself if you lack space). Using your sword, dagger or index finger, draw a Unicursal Hexagram in front of you in the air. Start at the upper tip, to the right, as shown in the following figure.

Unicursal Hexagram

To help you draw the Hexagram, once again you'll use your body as a guide. Start at your forehead and draw the first side down to your right side. From there, go up to your left shoulder and then down to your lower abdomen. Now go up to the right shoulder, then move to your left side, and finally up to your forehead to finish.

Visualize as you draw the Hexagram that a flame burst from the tip of your sword (dagger or index finger), such as the flame of a welding torch. This light must be visualized in extremely bright golden flames.

Now make the Sign of the Enterer. Inhale and absorb the energy, while bringing your hands to either side of your head, pointing the sword and your fingers forward. When exhaling, move one step forward, with your left foot, and thrust both hands in the center of the Hexagram. While doing so, vibrate the power word:

LIPVILLIT (Leh-peh-veh-leh-leh-tah)

This magickal word of power is composed of the first letter of each word of the following Enochian phrase, which means:

L I PAM VOVIN I LIALPRT L I TOFGLO

"One Is The Beginning, The Dragon Is The First Flame,
One Is Everything."

Feel the energy of this Divine name travelling out of your body, passing through your hands, into the precise center of the Hexagram. Return to your previous position and join your feet again, but keep your sword (dagger or index finger) still pointing at the center of the Hexagram. Then, draw a line of light in the air, walking along the outskirts of your circle, to the South. Visualize this line of a vivid white. The latter will connect all your Hexagrams together.

Facing the South, draw another Unicursal Hexagram. Then make the Sign of the Enterer while vibrating:

LIPVILLIT (Leh-peh-veh-leh-leh-tah)

Carry the line of white light to the West. Trace another Unicursal Hexagram and make the Sign of the Enterer while vibrating:

LIPVILLIT (Leh-peh-veh-leh-leh-tah)

Now head to the North carrying the white line. Facing North, trace the last Hexagram. Make the Sign of the Enterer and vibrate:

LIPVILLIT (Leh-peh-veh-leh-leh-tah)

Return to your starting point in the East, completing this circle of light. Then return to your initial position in the center of the magickal circle and face East. You are now surrounded by four Hexagrams of extremely bright golden flames. These are sealed by the power word, while being connected by a line of the purest light.

Right now, you should be able to see your four golden Hexagrams overlapped over four electric blue Pentagrams (from the Draconic Cross ritual), all joined together by a pure sphere of white light. Visualize the result obtained shining bright with incredible intensity and powerfully pulsating.

Part Two: The Draconic Cross

Repeat the first part of the Draconic Cross.

Touch your forehead and vibrate: **ZAH**
Point down and vibrate: **ONDOH**
Touch your right shoulder and vibrate: **MIH**
Touch your left shoulder and vibrate: **BUZD**
Then join hands and vibrate: **PAID, STELOI**

The ritual is now complete.

*
**

SUMMARY OF THE DRACONIC HEXAGRAM RITUAL

To help you memorize this rite, here's a summary without the explanations relating to visualization.

- *Part One: The formulation of the Hexagrams*

    Trace the Hexagram to the East. Vibrate: **LIPVILLIT**
    Trace the Hexagram to the South. Vibrate: **LIPVILLIT**
    Trace the Hexagram to the West. Vibrate: **LIPVILLIT**
    Trace the Hexagram to the North. Vibrate: **LIPVILLIT**

- *Part Two: The Draconic Cross*

    Touch your forehead and vibrate: **ZAH**
    Point down and vibrate: **ONDOH**
    Touch your right shoulder and vibrate: **MIH**
    Touch your left shoulder and vibrate: **BUZD**
    Then join hands and vibrate: **PAID, STELOI**

THE DRACONIC OPENING RITUAL

T HE Opening Ritual is a basic rite which consists in calling and invoking the magickal power of the four Watchtowers and its draconic Kings. You should practice it before any type of ceremony from the Draconia. This ritual will allow you to carry out the necessary preparations to dedicate your Draconic Temple of Magick and raise the vibratory atmosphere in order to invoke the presence of the great Draconic Force and that of its wise ministers. Very intense will be felt the energies after its practice; your workplace will be charged with the extraordinary intensity of dragon power.

You will also notice that this ritual is no more than a single complete ritual, which was divided into two distinct parts: Opening and Closing. The first part, used as a preliminary for all ceremonies of Draconia, is intended to evoke the Draconic Force. This is the perfect time to call upon dragons for support and assistance, while the second part of the rite will serve for concluding and blessing. When all the work has been done and completed, it will be time to return the energies back to where they came and give thanks to the dragons for their help.

Thus, whenever you want to undertake a draconic ceremony, you should always begin by banishing the negative influences from your immediate surroundings with the Draconic Cross, then move on to the Hexagram ritual, then the Opening Ritual. Once finished, you will be able to go directly to the practice of any occult experiments of your liking, including personal or draconic rites, divinatory sessions or other magickal works, etc.

Finally, when the time comes to complete your work, you will close your Temple and put an end to your Magick by performing the Closing Ritual. This is, ideally (but not mandatory), how a full draconic ceremony should take place.

Moreover, as you are a daraco, you can modify certain parts of this rite according to your inspiration and judgment, in that it will be possible to change it in accordance with your intimate and personal way of practicing Magick if needed be. Draconic Magick is permissive.

On a final note, please don't panic if you have difficulty memorizing the ritual by heart, this is quite normal, especially if you are on your first attempts. You can always provide a free space on your altar to place your personal grimoire, where the entire procedure would be carefully transcribed. Over time, you will find that your ritual conduct has become much more fluid as you have managed to memorize it entirely. Eventually, you'll hardly feel the need look at your notes. Fortunately, by then, the daraco's grimoire will be a valuable tool.

So, stay as determined and remember; because this ritual will now be explained in every detail, it may seem endless at first. However, if you read the summary carefully at the end, you will no doubt notice that it's much shorter than it looks and simpler than you have probably thought.

Remember: The Opening Ritual uses the ceremonial sword. If you don't have this noble magickal tool at hand, you can either craft one (as explained in the chapter about magickal tools) or temporarily use your draconic dagger as a substitute. The results obtained will be equally convincing.

The altar for the Draconic Opening Ritual

Place your altar facing East and set it up with all the needed tools for the ritual. Place your Fire Wand to the South, your Water Cup to the West, the Earth Pentacle to the North and the Air Dagger to the East. At the very center of the altar will rest the Draconic Pentacle and just above the Draconic Chalice filled with red wine. Finally, place a white candle at the right of the altar and a black at the left. The latter symbolizes the balance and union of the two main currents. You can also burn dragon's blood incense if you want to.

You will notice that when ready to dedicate your tools of Draconic Magick, the consecration ritual will require you to perform the Opening Rite beforehand. Don't worry, you will be able to use your tools for this ritual, even if they are not charged yet and duly consecrated. For each in their turn, they will be at the end of the ceremony.

Also, remember to take with you all the necessary equipment for any upcoming work you'll want to do afterwards, once the opening is complete. If you have previously done the Draconic Cross Ritual (which you should normally take the good habit of doing, your Magick circle will already be traced. If not, draw a circle, mentally or with the tip of your sword (dagger or index finger of the dominant hand) starting from the East. You are now ready to begin the Opening Rite.

*
**

THE OPENING RITE

Facing East, take place behind your altar table and say:

By the great Draconic Power, this Temple is now sealed.

Then light both candles. If you have a ritual bell, ring it ten times as follows:

/// //// ///

Each "/" corresponds to a bell ringing. If you don't have one, just use the pommel of your sword (or dagger) to gently strike the ten strokes against the altar as shown above. It is now time to declare the opening of the ritual by pronouncing aloud:

HEKAS, HEKAS, ESTE BEBELOI!
(Hay-kas, Hay-kas, Ehs-teeh, Bee-bee-loy)

This traditional magickal phrase indicates the ritual is now underway and that all unwanted Entities (physical and invisible), who are not allowed to attend, must therefore promptly leave the draconic Temple.
Now point the sword at the Draconic Pentacle and say:

Draconis, draconis, draconis!
Dragons of Spirit, wise and strong,
Transfer your power on this altar,

And bless it with your fiery breath,
May we be as One in Draconia,
O dragons wise and immortal.

The Great Southern Quadrangle

Take a short break, then grab your Fire Wand. Always behind the altar, turn to face South. Visualize a pure and brilliant fire irradiating from the Wand. Then give three soft blows in the air, left, right, and center. Then say, holding your Wand high in the air:

And when, after all the phantoms have vanished,
Thou shalt see that holy and formless Fire,
That Fire which darts and flashes through the hidden depths of the universe,
Hear thou the voice of Fire.

Wand in hand, move clockwise around the circle to the South. Trace the Invoking Pentagram of Fire with your Wand (as you learned during the Draconic Cross) starting with the point indicated by the arrow in the following figure.

Visualize this Pentagram in flaming red. Then point the Wand at the center and vibrate:

OIP-TEAA-PDOKE
(Oh-ee-peh-Teh-ah-ah-Peh-doh-keh)

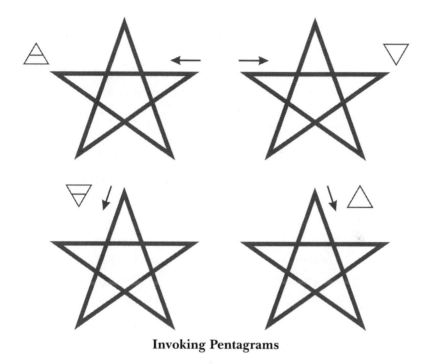

Invoking Pentagrams

Finally, raise your wand over your head and say:

In the draconic names and powers of the Great Southern Quadrangle, I invoke ye, ye Fiery Dragons of the Watchtower of the South.

Take a few moments to feel and see from this quarter, this pure elemental energy charged by the power of the Fire dragons. Then, clockwise walk back behind your altar and replace the Wand.

The Great Western Quadrangle

Now take your Water Cup and face West. With your fingers, sprinkle some water droplets in this direction, left, right, and center. Then say, raising the Cup to the sky:

So therefore first, the Daraco who governeth the works of Fire must sprinkle with the lustral water of the loud resounding sea.

Then circumambulate West (always clockwise) around the circle. Trace the Invoking Pentagram of Water, using the Cup, visualizing it in electric blue. Then point the Cup at the center of the Pentagram and vibrate:

MPH-ARSL-GAIOL
(Em-peh-heh-Ar-ess-el-Gah-eh-oh-leh)

Finally, hold the Cup on high and add:

In the draconic names and powers of the Great Western Quadrangle, I invoke ye, ye Dragons of the Watchtower of the West.

Take a few moments to feel and see from this quarter, this pure elemental energy charged by the power of the Water dragons. Then, walk back to your altar and replace the Cup.

THE GREAT EASTERN QUADRANGLE

Take your Air Dagger and face East. Strike the air three times, left, right, and center. Then say, holding the Dagger on high:

Such a Fire existeth, extending through the rushing of Air. Or even a Fire formless, whence cometh the image of a voice. Or even a flashing light, abounding, revolving, whirling forth, crying aloud.

Then circumambulate East around the circle. Trace the Invoking Pentagram of Air, using the dagger. Visualizing it in bright yellow. Then point the blade at the center of the Pentagram and vibrate:

ORO-IBAH-AOZPI
(Oh-roh-Eh-bah-Ah-oh-zod-peh)

Finally, raise the dagger and add:

In the draconic names and powers of the Great Eastern Quadrangle, I invoke ye, ye Dragons of the Watchtower of the East.

Take a few moments to feel and see from this quarter, this pure elemental energy charged by the power of the Air dragons. Then, return to your altar and replace the Dagger.

The Great Northern Quadrangle

Take the Earth Pentacle and face North. Strike the air three times towards this direction, left, right, and center. Then say, presenting the Pentacle on high before you:

Stoop not down into that darkly splendid world wherein continually lieth a faithless depth and Hades wrapped in gloom, delighting in unintelligible images, precipitous, winding: A black ever-rolling abyss, ever espousing a body unluminous, formless and void.

Then circumambulate North. Trace the Invoking Pentagram of Earth using the Pentacle and visualize it in electric green. Then point it at the center of the Pentagram and vibrate:

MOR-DIAL-HKTGA
(Moh-ar-Dee-ah-leh-Heh-keh-teh-gah)

Finally, raise the Pentacle on high as you add:

In the draconic names and powers of the Great Northern Quadrangle, I invoke ye, ye Dragons of the Watchtower of the North.

Take a few moments to feel and see from this quarter, this pure elemental energy charged by the power of the Earth dragons. Then replace the Pentacle on the altar.

The Call to Draconic Power

Face East. Now take your sword with both hands and kneel. Meditate in silence a few moments, mentally connect yourself to the Draconic Force and dragons. Rise up afterwards, point the sword at the Draconic Pentacle and say:

Draconis! Draconis! Draconis!
Draconic Kings, FAFNYR, NAËLYAN, SAIRYS, GRAËL,
Sovereign Dragons and all beings from the Draconia.
Come all. Come, haste and listen.

Me (your magickal name), **Daraco in search of truth and Dragons, In quest of esoteric knowledge and draconic power, I, the Daraco and Priest of the Great and Mystic Draconia, I now enter the Draconic Kingdom with your blessing. O Ancient and most Wise Dragons, come, haste and listen.**

Vibrate:
ELEXARPH COMANANU TABITOM
Zodacare, eca, od zodameranu.
Odo cicale Qaa: piap Piamoel od Vaoan!

The last segment means:
"(Three great magickal names reigning over elemental energies.)
Come forward, come and appear.
Open the mysteries of creation: balance, righteousness and truth!"

These words of power are pronounced as follows:

El-ehtz-ar-peh-eh, Coh-mah-nah-noo, Tah-bee-toh-meh.
Zod-ah-kah-reh, Eh-kah, Oh-deh Zod-ah-meh-rah-noo.
Oh-doh Keh-kah-leh Quah-ah: Pee-ah-peh Pee-ah-moh-el
Oh-deh Vah-oh-ah-en!

Visualize the elemental energies blending all together, feeling the greatness of the Draconic Force bursting from everywhere, in all directions. This palpable energy is embracing and penetrating you completely. The Opening Rite is complete. The whole Draconia is present. Dragons are here, by your side, waiting your command.

It's now time to perform any type of rituals, spells, Dragon Magick, meditation exercises, divination or any other occult work you may want to do. This is also the perfect time to get in touch with your familiar dragons and ask them questions or their help.

When you're finished with your rituals and other magickal practices, it will be time to close your draconic Temple by performing the Closing Ritual. You will thus send all energies back to their respective realms. Don't forget thanking the dragons for their service.

*
**

SUMMARY OF THE DRACONIC OPENING RITUAL

To help you memorize this rite, here's a summary without the explanations relating to visualization.

- *The Opening Rite*

    By the great Draconic Power, this circle is now sealed.
    Ring the bell ten times: /// //// ///
    HEKAS, HEKAS, ESTE BEBELOI!
    Point the sword at the Draconic Pentacle and say:
    Draconis, draconis, draconis!
    Dragons of Spirit, wise and strong, transfer your power on this altar, and bless it with your fiery breath, may we be as One in Draconia, O dragons wise and immortal.

- *The Great Southern Quadrangle*

    Take the Fire Wand and strike the air three times. Say:
    And when, after all the phantoms have vanished, thou shalt see that holy and formless Fire, that Fire which darts and flashes through the hidden depths of the universe, hear thou the voice of Fire.
    Go South. Trace the Invoking Pentagram of Fire.
    Point the center and vibrate: **OIP-TEAA-PDOKE**
    Raise the wand and say:
    In the draconic names and powers of the Great Southern Quadrangle, I invoke ye, ye Fiery Dragons of the Watchtower of the South.

- *The Great Western Quadrangle*

  Sprinkle some water droplets in the West. Say:
  **So therefore first, the Daraco who governeth the
  works of Fire must sprinkle with the lustral water of
  the loud resounding sea.**
  Walk West and trace Invoking Pentagram of Water.
  Point the center and vibrate: **MPH-ARSL-GAIOL**
  Hold the Cup on high and add:
  **In the draconic names and powers of the Great
  Western Quadrangle, I invoke ye, ye Dragons of the
  Watchtower of the West.**

- *The Large Eastern Quadrangle*

  Strike the air three times with the Dagger, then say:
  **Such a Fire existeth, extending through the rushing
  of Air. Or even a Fire formless, whence cometh the
  image of a voice. Or even a flashing light, abounding,
  revolving, whirling forth, crying aloud.**
  Walk East and trace the Invoking Pentagram of Air.
  Point the center and vibrate: **ORO-IBAH-AOZPI**
  Raise the dagger and add:
  **In the draconic names and powers of the Great
  Eastern Quadrangle, I invoke ye, ye Dragons of the
  Watchtower of the East.**

- *The Great Northern Quadrangle*

  Strike the air three times with the Pentacle and say:
  Stoop not down into that darkly splendid world

wherein continually lieth a faithless depth and
Hades wrapped in gloom, delighting in unintelligible
images, precipitous, winding: A black ever-rolling
abyss, ever espousing a body unluminous, formless
and void.

Walk North. Trace the Invoking Pentagram of Earth.
Point the center and vibrate: **MOR-DIAL-HKTGA**
Hold the Pentacle on high and add:

In the draconic names and powers of the Great
Northern Quadrangle, I invoke ye, ye Dragons of the
Watchtower of the North.

- *The Call to Draconic Power*

Hold the sword and kneel. Meditate.
Rise up and point the sword at the Draconic Pentacle:
Draconis! Draconis! Draconis!
Draconic Kings, FAFNYR, NAËLYAN, SAIRYS,
GRAËL. Sovereign Dragons and all beings from the
Draconia. Come all. Come, haste and listen.
Me (your magickal name), **Daraco in search of truth**
and Dragons. In quest of esoteric knowledge and
draconic power, I, the Daraco and Priest of the Great
and Mystic Draconia, I now enter the Draconic
Kingdom with your blessing. O Ancient and Most
Wise Dragons, come, haste and listen.
Vibrate: **ELEXARPH COMANANU TABITOM**
Zodacare, eca, od zodameranu.
Odo cicale Qaa: piap Piamoel od Vaoan!

- *Perform your Draconic Magick.*

THE DRACONIC CLOSING RITUAL

WHEN your ceremony has come to an end, that all your Draconic Magick work has been accomplished, it will be time to conclude using the following Closing Rite.

Circumambulate your circle three times widdershins. As you do, feel the energies gradually lifting, dissipate and evaporate. Back at your altar, raise your Draconic Chalice and solemnly say:

> **Power Chalice, Draconic Reservoir of Knowledge, Transfer the Wisdom and Light poured by Dragons unto the daraco who drinks you!**

Carry the cup to your lips and slowly drink its contents, visualizing that you absorb all the energies graced by dragons. Feel this warm and peaceful feeling of power empowering your whole body. Finally, replace the Chalice, and right hand on the heart, say:

> **Unto you, Wise, Eternal, unto you Mighty Dragons, I thank thee for partaking your wisdom,**

And shared your most great Spiritual and Magical Knowledge.
Come back to this Draconic Temple on my next call,
Here, in this Sanctuary dedicated to the most High Draconia.
Forever be glorified by the Light and go in peace.
Draconis! Draconis! Draconis!

Ring the bell (or strike the pommel) ten times:

/// //// ///

Then say:

I now declare this sacred Temple of Draconic Magick duly closed.

Strike one last blow with the sword pommel.
Give the Triple Sign and extinguish the candles.

RITES OF PASSAGE OF DRACONIA

R ITES of Passage are initiation rituals used since time immemorial by practitioners of different cultures to dedicate themselves to the magickal, spiritual or religious path. The following ritual will be very important for you, because it means you wish, of your own volition, to solemnly swear allegiance to the Draconic Code and be initiated to Draconia, under the supervision and approval of the dragons.

Among the different levels of Draconic Magick initiation, this ritual is the very first you will pass. As you gain more experience over time, and gradually show greater personal and magickal mastery of Universal Laws, you will be entitled to advance to the second initiatory degree, and so on.

The first degree ritual is often referred to as *Entering the Dragon's Lair*. This means you will present yourself in the depths of their sanctuary, pure of heart, and ask to be accepted as a newcomer on the path of Draconia, as a draconic magician. It will also be the point of no return, because once in the Lair, you will be judged. If you are not sufficiently prepared, you will be denied access and will be asked to leave the premises immediately. On the other hand, if you pass this initiatory rite and succeed in proving yourself, you will then be a true daraco (at the rank of neophyte), recognized by the whole brotherhood of draconic Beings.

You will see for yourself that the Rite of Passage is a great moment filled with emotions and mysteries. You will for sure experience something extraordinary that will remain in your memory forever. Also, note that Initiation Rites are not necessarily rituals that can only be performed once. In fact, as soon as you have been promoted to your first initiatory rank, you will be able to practice the same ritual as often as you wish, in order to tangibly reaffirm your commitments or, simply, to feel once again this peaceful and strong feeling of bliss provided by this exchange of energy between you and dragons. Repeating a Rite of Passage is a bit like going to visit, from time to time, your old friends and fellow dragons...

As mentioned earlier, those who practice the teachings of Dragon Magick usually tend to work alone. Draconia will always remain, above all else, a personal magickal and spiritual discipline. This is why this magnificent ritual, that has been offered to us by the dragons, must be performed alone. If you feel ready, then proceed without fear and enter the Lair.

First Vradysconn:
LET THE NEOPHYTE STEP FORWARD...

Start by performing the Draconic Cross ritual, followed by the Hexagram ritual, then the Opening ritual. As soon as the Opening Rite is completed and the Draconic Force and dragons are standing by your side, sit comfortably behind your altar. You can even lie down if you wish. Now close your eyes and completely relax your body and mind.

Visualize you're walking a winding path on a beautiful starry night. The moon is full and shines bright. Your steps are slow and steady. This trail is marked by small stones from which emanates a faint white glow illuminating your steps. As you move forward, you feel this strong attraction towards a luminous spot in the distance.

Finally, after a while, you reach the side of a majestic mountain. In front of you, you can see the features of a gigantic cave which, surprisingly, made in the shape of a dragon's mouth; this is the *Lair of Initiation*. As you silently approach the entrance, your eyes perceive a reddish glow that seems to come directly from the bowels of the Earth, far into the unknown depths of human consciousness. Entering the earthly entrails, you continue on a downward slope, while the presence of dragons is felt more and more strongly. You go down, down, down ever deeper...

You are now bathing in a bright red aura. You can't, for the moment, know where this light comes from, because it's so ubiquitous, as if the air you're breathing itself is tinged with red. As you continue your descent, which seems to last for a very long time already, finally right in front of you, at the very bottom of this cave, stands a huge golden door. You can examine a finely engraved sign that reads:

—————————{ *What is thou seekest ?* }—————————

Mentally you answer:
Pure of heart, I am the one who aspires to know the mysteries of Draconia.

At this point, if dragons decide you are not ready, nothing will happen and the door will remain firmly shut. You will only have to turn back and return to the path leading to the outside world. Come back another time and do some introspection to find out where you have failed.

If dragons find you worthy, then slowly and without any squeaking, the door will open wide, letting shine out from behind, this strong, intense and warm, red and pulsating light, blinding you momentarily and enveloping your whole body. You experience a feeling of purity that you have never experienced before.

As your eyes slowly become accustomed to this light that penetrates and surrounds you, you take a step forward and cross the threshold. You are now inside a huge circular room. You see crystals embedded in the rocky walls. Long dragon-like tapestries hang from the four Watchtowers. At the other end, on a very large and imposing stone altar finely chiseled, rests a magnificent red crystal chalice of inestimable value. You now understand where this powerful luminosity originates; as bright as thousands of suns, indescribable, radiating a blinding light all around you, to the deepest of your soul; *this magnificent light comes directly from the cup.*

You feel a warmth, which in normal times would be simply unbearable but strange as it may seem, you feel extremely well and completely at ease. You move toward the altar. Stealth shadows hover above your head. Some of them give the impression of swirling by describing large circles around you; it's the dragons. You then stop in front of the altar to contemplate the crystal cup. Never have you seen such a beautiful and precious object.

Breathe deeply and say aloud:
By my own free will, I came for Initiation.
By this Rite of Passage and under the approval of Dragons,
I solemnly pledge allegiance to the Draconic Code.
May I be accepted within Draconia.

After a short moment of silence, a voice full of wisdom, almost unspeakable, will be heard and pronounce:

"Drink the content of the Cup."

Do as you are told and respectfully take the chalice with both hands. Slowly carry it to your lips and drink the liquid. At this moment, you feel the Draconic Force, this powerful energy of dragons, penetrating you and flowing vividly into your entire body. Take a few seconds to savor this moment, then in silence, replace the cup on the altar and solemnly give the Triple Sign with your right hand. Turn around, walk out of the room and take your leave. When you'll be outside back on the trail, stop and see if there's a dragon waiting for you, to share any information relevant to your evolution. Then slowly open your eyes...

Although you may feel this guided meditation was only happening in your head, out of your imagination, conveyed by your ability to visualize, but rest assured, the experience did occur and, indeed, was very real. Conclude the ceremony by performing the Closing Ritual. The Rite of Passage of the first degree of Draconia has just been completed. You have just been properly initiated to draconic practices. Please allow me to greet you fraternally with the Triple Sign.

Second Initiation Degree

H ERE is the Rite of Passage of the second initiatory degree of Draconia. You will be entitled to practice it only after you have gained more experience in Draconic Magick, knowing you have passed the first Rite of Passage and have been granted the status of *Daraco Neophyte*. This ritual, like the previous one, will be carried out once again by a journey of the mind into the Draconic Zone.

When you are ready to take a step further on the path of magickal and spiritual perfection, and feel ready to reach a higher level, you will then be able to return to the heart of Draconia to receive the second draconic rank called *Paetryn Daraco*, which is associated with the Cosmic Element of the Earth.

SECOND VRADYSCONN:
LET THE DARACO PROVE HIS PROGRESS...

Start by performing the Draconic Cross ritual, followed by the Hexagram ritual, then the Opening ritual. As soon as the Draconic Force and dragons have been summoned, sit comfortably behind your altar. You can even lie down if you wish. Now close your eyes and completely relax your mind and body.

Visualize that you are back on this winding path, the same you walked in the past, on a beautiful starry night. The moon is full and shines bright. Once again, your approach is slow and confident. This path is always marked by the same small stones from which emanates a faint white glow illuminating your steps. As you walk, you feel this strong attraction towards a bright spot that you see in the distance. Finally, after a while, you reach the side of this majestic mountain that you now well know. In front of you are the features of the *Lair of Initiation*, this huge cave surprisingly shaped like a dragon's mouth. As you silently approach the entrance, your eyes perceive a greenish glow that seems to come directly from the center of the Earth, far into the depths unknown to man. Entering the bowels of the Earth, you continue on this downward slope, as the presence of dragons is felt more and more strongly. You go down, down, down ever deeper...

You are now surrounded in a bright greenish aura. This light is omnipresent, as if the air you breathe were itself tinted in green. As you continue your descent, which seems to have been going on for a long time, you finally see, straight ahead of you, like a huge vestibule, a circular room with six massive and very high doors. You notice on the far left, the golden door of the first initiatory degree, which you have already crossed. Strangely, on your first visit, the other entrances did not seem to be present, as if they had been deliberately veiled to your eyes while you were still a profane.

You feel terribly drawn to the beautiful crystal door, the farthest from you, on your right. A feeling in you makes you realize the time has not yet come for you to approach it. You then turn your attention to the greenish door; this is the one that awaits you. As you approach it, you can study a finely engraved sign that reads:

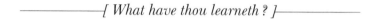

—————————{ *What have thou learneth ?* }—————————

Mentally you answer:

I am the apprentice Daraco who implements the Universal Laws of the One, I apply the Draconic Code and the teachings of Draconia.

At this point, if dragons decide your magickal or spiritual progress has been only superficial, nothing will happen and the door will remain firmly closed. You'll have no choice but to walk back up the path leading you to the outside world. Come back another day and take the time to introspect to find out where you have failed.

If, on the other hand, dragons consider you have progressed admirably, then slowly and without any noises, the door will open wide, letting this strong and intense green and pulsating light burst outside the room, blinding you momentarily and enveloping your whole body. You feel an indescribable feeling.

As your eyes slowly become accustomed to this luminosity penetrating and surrounding your entire being, proceed, step forward and cross the threshold. You are now inside a huge circular room. The ceiling is extremely high. Looking down, you see an impressive circled pentagram engraved on the floor. On each of its points stands a very large green dragon. They are quietly looking at you. Silent. As you turn your attention to the walls, you notice, hung on each of the four Watchtowers, long emerald tapestries, evoking dragons interlaced on pentagrams. Right in front of you, in the center of the five-pointed star, is an imposing and finely chiseled stone altar on which shines a magnificent pentacle of inestimable value, carved from a large emerald. You now understand where this powerful light originates; as bright as thousands of suns, indescribable, radiating a blinding light all around you, to the deepest of your soul; *this magnificent light comes directly from the pentacle.*

The air is highly charged with vibrations. As you advance towards the altar, the dragons, as impassive as eternal guardians, simply turn around, constantly facing you; their wide eyes watching the smallest of your movements. You stop in front of the altar to contemplate the pentacle. Never have you seen such a beautiful and precious object.

Now, take a deep breath and say aloud:
By my own free will, I came for Initiation.
By this Second Rite of Passage and under the approval of Dragons,
May my efforts ennoble my self, heart and soul,
To magically and spiritually elevate me as a brother in Draconia.

After a moment of silence, a voice full of wisdom, almost unspeakable, will be heard and pronounce:

"Place your hand on the Pentacle."

Do as you are told and slowly put your right hand on the emerald pentacle. At this same moment, you feel the Draconic Force, this powerful energy of dragons, penetrating you and flowing vividly into your entire body.

After a moment of pure bliss, bathing in this invigorating energy, solemnly give the Triple Sign facing each green dragon, clockwise in their turn, starting with the one facing you, at the upper point of the pentagram. Then turn around, walk out of the room and take your leave. When you'll be outside, back on the trail, stop and see if there's a dragon waiting for you, to share any information relevant to your evolution. Then slowly open your eyes...

Complete the ceremony with the Closing Ritual. The Rite of Passage of the second degree of Draconia has just been concluded. You are now *Paetryn Daraco*, a draconic magician at the stage of "learning". Congratulations!

 # THIRD INITIATION DEGREE

T HE third Initiation degree of Draconia is the last Rite of Passage of this book. I have already mentioned there are three others, which is true; the most advanced that will be practiced differently from those you already know. However, these cannot be revealed to you at this time. Before being able to obtain the last draconic degrees, a lot of personal work will have to be undertaken. Now, if you progress on the magickal path in a blazing way, which may be the case for some serious students, perhaps these rites will even be transmitted directly to you by one of your familiar dragons. This is my wish for you. If not, I will be able to disclose them to you, only when the time is right, in a forthcoming book on advanced draconic teachings.

You will be entitled to pass this Initiation Rite only when you have acquired a certain mastery in Magick as well as in the application of draconic teachings, knowing of course you have passed the second Rite of Passage beforehand, granted you have earned the grade of *Paetryn Daraco*. This ritual, like the previous ones, will be carried out by a new journey of the mind into the Draconic Zone.

The initiation of the third draconic degree will give you the vradysconn *Aether Daraco*. The latter is associated with the Cosmic Element of Air.

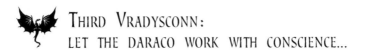

THIRD VRADYSCONN:
LET THE DARACO WORK WITH CONSCIENCE...

Start by performing the Draconic Cross ritual, followed by the Hexagram ritual, then the Opening ritual. As soon as the Draconic Force and dragons have been summoned, sit comfortably behind your altar. You can even lie down if you wish. Now close your eyes and relax completely your mind and body.

Visualize you're once again walking on this winding path now very familiar to you. It's night and the stars are shining in the sky. There's a beautiful full moon. A gentle breeze caresses your face. This path is marked by the same small stones from which emanates a faint white glow illuminating your steps. As you walk, you feel this strong attraction towards a bright spot in the distance. You know you're here for a very important reason: a Rite of Passage. Finally, you reach the side of the *Lair of Initiation*, this huge cave in the shape of a dragon's mouth you know too well. As you silently approach the entrance, your eyes perceive a yellowish glow that seems to come directly from the center of the Earth, far into the unknown depths of human consciousness. Entering the bowels of the Earth, you continue on this downward slope, as the presence of dragons is felt more and more strongly. You go down, down, down ever deeper...

You are now wrapped in a bright yellowish aura. This light is omnipresent, as if the very air you breathe were itself tinted in yellow. As you continue your descent, which seems to last for a very long time already, you see in front of you a circular room, this immense vestibule with its six massive doors of the initiatory thresholds. You notice the doors that previously opened to you, the golden door of the first degree to your left, followed by the second door gleaming with an indescribable green.

You feel more than ever this attraction, this need to cross the threshold of the magnificent crystal gate, the farthest from you, on your right. You still have this same feeling as before, making you realize that time has not yet come to try it. So, you turn your attention to the yellow door; this is the one that awaits you. As you approach it, you can read a finely engraved sign that reads:

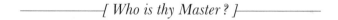
———————{ *Who is thy Master?* }———————

Mentally you answer:
I am the humble Daraco in training, at the service of the One. I am the one who works with conscience according to the Universal Laws and the teachings of Draconia.

At this point, if dragons decide your motives are egoistic or you show no respect for the Draconic Code, nothing will happen and the door will remain firmly closed. You'll have no choice but to turn around and walk back up the path leading you to the outside world. Come back another day and take the time to introspect to find out where you have failed.

If, on the other hand, dragons deem your motives to be noble and you have once again proved your awakened state of consciousness, then slowly and without any noise, the door will open wide, letting this strong and intense yellowish and pulsating light burst outside the room, blinding you momentarily and enveloping your whole body. You experience an indescribable feeling, as if you were suddenly very light, as you cross the threshold.

To your amazement, you are no longer inside the mountain, deep in the Lair of Initiation, but rather outside on its summit. From the top of the mountain, the sky is still slightly dark, but it gives a glimpse of a coming dawn. Stars are always present, like small sparkling diamonds far above. Looking around, you realize you are not alone. You see several Air dragons constantly moving, flying and swirling around where you stand. These draconic Entities are your witnesses. They are the ones who granted you access to the third door and will assist you during this Initiation Passage. While remaining silent, they indicate to look before you. A dagger standing on the tip of the blade, as if floating almost in a state of weightlessness, rests on a superb finely chiseled stone altar. That bright powerful yellow light, that dazzled you not long ago, was actually emanate directly from this object.

As you move towards the altar, the Air dragons pursue what looks like a dance, floating here and there while looking at you with great attention. Never have you seen such a beautiful dagger; it just looks extraordinary to you. Now breathe deeply and say aloud:

By my own free will, I came for Initiation.
By this Third Rite of Passage and under the approval
of Dragons,
May my mind remain awake and conscious at all
times,
And may my actions reflect the will of the One in
accordance with Draconia.

After a moment of silence, a voice full of wisdom, almost unspeakable, will be heard and pronounce:

"Hold the Dagger."

Do as you are told. The very moment where, dagger in hand, you hold it high towards the sky, you feel the Draconic Force, the powerful energy of dragons, penetrating you and flowing vividly through your entire body. After a short time, replace the dagger on the altar and solemnly give the Triple Sign. Turn around, your back to the altar; you now see one of the majestic Air dragons facing you. As he approaches in silence, you can feel the goodness emanating from his eyes. You are so moved that it becomes difficult to hold your emotions. He gently lifts a paw and places it softly on your forehead. As soon as he touches you, you automatically find yourself back in the vestibule, in the heart of the mountain. You're once again facing the third initiatory door, now closed, where you were previously, before it opened all wide to you, only moments ago.

As you walk your way back to the surface, you fully understand why your fellow dragon didn't just teleport you on the outside path. He wanted you to walk all the way up on your own, so you understand that mastering Magick is a long road where there are no shortcuts.

Once outside the cave, back on the path, stop and see if there's a dragon waiting for you, to share any information relevant to your evolution. Then open your eyes...

Complete the ceremony with the Closing Ritual. The Rite of Passage of the third degree of Draconia has just been concluded. You are now *Aether Daraco*, a draconic magician at the stage of a "conscious awakening of mastery." Well done!

CALLING UPON FAMILIAR DRAGONS

ALL daracos should have at least one familiar drag-on or rather, should I say, be assigned an assistant. Since dragons are free beings just like you and I, and no one has the right to try to force them into obedi-ence. Once you have gained any experience in Draconic Magick, you will be able to practice the Familiar Dragon ritual. This Major Rite consists in asking the supreme pow-er, the One, to assign you one, or (eventually) several drag-ons, to assist you throughout your draconic career.

The benefits will be far more than substantial; they will simply be countless. Either to permanently step into the draconic world as or be in contact with these Beings, day after day, I recommend you perform this ritual as soon as it will be possible for you to practice it skillfully. Not only will your familiar be protecting you from invisible astral forces and warn you of impending dangers, whether on the material plane and during astral travels (a privileged moment to communicate and journey with your dragon), but it turns out that, depending on his level of maturity in the *Chain of Wisdom*, he can be just as favorable to you during your occult works.

Make sure you are alone for at least an hour to complete the ceremony.

*
**

MAJOR RITE OF THE FAMILIAR DRAGON

PART ONE: THE DRACONIC STAR

Perform the Draconic Cross ritual.
Perform the Draconic Hexagram ritual
Perform the Opening ritual.

It is mandatory to perform the preliminary rituals in order to, firstly, banish any hostile and psychic influences, then, secondly, to adjust your workplace the right vibratory frequency.

Facing East, declare in a solemn and humble tone:

O Thou, Eternal Cosmic Light who is Mother and Father of all things, Thou who drape the forces of nature and the Universe, I therefore ask Thy Holy presence.
O Thou, Eternal Draconic Force born form the One, by whom Thou manifest yourself, Thou who shines and vibrates through all things, I ask Thee to be assigned a Familiar Dragon who will be my companion and faithful assistant; a brave and wise

Draconic Guardian, for the time that will be allotted to me.

Let him come to me, free of choice, and manifest himself in the names of Draconia and the One.

Again, I humbly ask, as a disciple of Draconia and of Cosmic Laws, and by the approval of the Draconic Kings, that a Familiar Dragon be granted unto me, here and now, to serve as a protective guide and assist me in my personal, magickal and spiritual quest.

Now walk to the boundaries of your circle facing East (circle that was originally traced by the Draconic Cross) and draw in the air, in front of you, an *Active* Draconic Star (Heptagram) starting at the point indicated, in a continuous and fluid line, while vibrating:

VOVIN-DRACONIS (Voh-vee-neh-Drah-coh-nis)

Active Draconic Heptagram   **Passive Draconic Heptagram**

Visualize this star in a bright, pulsating and extremely vivid purple. Make the Sign of the enterer while pronouncing the last syllable (*Drrahh-cooohh-niih*-SSSS) by thrusting both hands into the center of the star, as you already do during the Rite of the Draconic Cross.

To summarize this new procedure, the vibration of the magickal name will last all exhalation, from the moment you start tracing the symbol, until the Sign of the Enterer. This means you need to take a deep breath to get enough air as you dive your hands forcefully into the center of the Draconic Star.

Line of Light connecting the draconic Heptagrams

Feel the energy of that name going out of your body, traveling through your hands, into the Heptagram. Then return to your initial position and draw a line heading south. Visualize this line of light in a very bright white. The latter will connect all your stars together by their center.

To the South; trace another *Active* Draconic Heptagram, always in vivid purple, while vibrating:

VOVIN-DRACONIS (Voh-vee-neh-Drah-coh-nis)

Again, make the Sign of the Enterer by thrusting your hands into the center of the heptagram wile exhaling the last syllable. Feel the energy of that name traveling out of your body, through your hands, into the Draconic Star. Return to your position, then draw the white line of light to the West.

Facing the Western Quarter, trace the *Passive* Draconic Heptagram, always in sparkling purple, while vibrating:

VOVIN-DRACONIS (Voh-vee-neh-Drah-coh-nis)

Make the Sign of the Enterer and feel the energy of this name go through your whole body, as before. Then draw the line heading North.

To the North, trace the *Passive* Draconic Heptagram while vibrating:

VOVIN-DRACONIS (Voh-vee-neh-Drah-coh-nis)

Make the Sign of the Enterer one last time and feel the energy of the name. Finally, seal the circle of light as you circumambulate East, returning to your starting point.

Take your original position in the center of the magick circle and face East. You are now circled by four draconic Heptagrams of a very bright electric purple. These are connected by a line of the pure white light.

Part Two: The Astral Manifestation

Take three deep breaths, focus on the goal of the ritual, and then, with your right hand on your heart, say aloud:

O Thou, Eternal Draconic Force born form the One, by whom Thou manifest yourself, Thou who shines and vibrates through all things, I ask Thee to be assigned a Familiar Dragon, here and now, in this Draconic Temple.
For the time that will be allotted to me, as a disciple of Draconia and of Cosmic Laws, let a faithful and Familiar Dragon be granted unto me, here and now, to serve as a protective guide and assist me in my personal, magickal and spiritual quest.
Let him come to me, free of choice.
Dragon: manifest, manifest, manifest!

Take a short break in silence and remain passive while waiting for an astral manifestation. After a while, raise your right hand with your palm extended forward and continue:

**OL LRING-ILS THEY GAH VOVIN DO TOFGLO DS
CHIS DOOAIN BUSD OD MICALZO IAD DRILPA
DS I DRILPI OMP.
NIIS: CHRISTEOS FAORGT AFFA.
IMVAMAR LAIAD OD GNAY NANAEEL.
ZAMRAN PUJO-OOANOAN, GOHOL LAIAD DO-
BIAN OD DO-OMP.
VOVIN ZAMRAN PUJO-OOANOAN,
ZAMRAN PUJO-OOANOAN,
ZAMRAN PUJO-OOANOAN!**

These words mean the following:

*I evoke you, O Dragon Spirit in all things which are the names
of glory and the power of the One god who is greater than
understanding.*
Come closer: leave your abode empty.
Apply yourself to the secret truth and do my power.
*Appear unto my eyes, speaking the secrets of truth, in voice
and understanding.*
Dragon, appear unto my eyes,
Appear unto my eyes,
Appear unto my eyes!

And they are pronounced:

*Oh-el Lah-reh-nuh-geh-Heh-lah-sah Heh-lah-sah Gah-heh
Voh-vee-neh Doh Toh-fah-geh-loh Dah-sah Cah-his Doh-hoh-
ah-heh-nu Bu-zod-deh Od Meh-cah-lah-zod-oh Eh-ah-dah
Dah-reh-lah-pah Dah-sah Eh Dreh-lah-peh Oh-mèh-pèh.*

Nee-eh-sah: Chris-the-os Fah-oh-re-geh-tah Ah-fah-fah.
Eh-mu-ah-mar Lah-eh-ah-dah Od Geh-nay Nah-nah-el.
Zodah-mran Pujoh-Oh-oh-ah-noh-an, Goh-oh-lah Lah-eh-ah-dah Doh-Beh-ah-nu Od Doh-Oh-mèh-pèh.
Voh-vee-neh Zodah-mran Pujoh-Oh-oh-ah-noh-an,
Zodah-mran Pujoh-Oh-oh-ah-noh-an,
Zodah-mran Pujoh-Oh-oh-ah-noh-an.

Wait in silence. When you will see the dragon appear and move towards you or when, at the very least, you are convinced that an astral draconic manifestation has taken place, give the Triple Sign and add, always in the same tone of voice:

VOVIN, NIIS ASPT A OD AR A, QUASB OD BABALON.
VOVIN, GOHO HAS ANANAEL OD FISIS IADNAH.
VOVIN, A NOQOL HOATH OD LONSHI, ODO A DRACONIA!

These words mean:

Dragon, come before me and protect me, destroy that is evil and malevolent.
Dragon, teach me the Secret Wisdow and perform your knowledge.
Dragon, my devoted and powerful Familiar, open my self to Draconia!

And are pronounced like so:

Voh-vee-neh, Nee-eh-ess Ah-seh-peh-teh Ah Od Are Ah, Quah-seh-beh Od Bah-bah-loh-en.
Voh-vee-neh, Goh-oh Ah Ah-nah-nah-el Od Feh-see-ess Eh-ah-deh-nah.
Voh-vee-neh, Ah Noh-quo-leh Hoh-ah-teh Od Loh-en-ess-hee, Oh-doh Ah Draconia!

PART THREE: THE INSTRUCTION AND DISCHARGE

If all went well, you should now be facing the dragon who will become your familiar and assistant magician. You might not necessarily have a need to communicate with him through speech, because all the discussion can be held mentally.

See what he has to communicate and then instruct him on how you want him to assist you in the future; on the ways he must answer your calls, and what could be the signals or special words of power to summon him. You might want, of course, to ask him to reveal his name, if he has not already done so, as well as inquiring him where he comes from and what is his level of maturity in the *Chain of Wisdom*, etc.

Once you have completed this third part of the ritual, it will be time to recite the discharge and bid farewell to your new companion so he may go back to him realm, until his presence is needed again.

Therefore, take a deep breath and say:

Go in peace, Familiar Dragon and assistant magician. You can return to your Sphere of origin. By my simple call, whether verbal or mental, come to me, haste, and listen to receive the instructions I will have to give you. May we be one in Draconia. Steloi!

Give the Triple Sign.
Practice the Closing Rite.

*
**

SUMMARY OF THE MAJOR RITE OF THE FAMILIAR DRAGON

- *Part One: The Draconic Star*

Perform the Draconic Cross ritual.
Perform the Draconic Hexagram ritual
Perform the Opening ritual.

Facing East:
O Thou, Eternal Cosmic Light who is Mother and Father of all things, Thou who drape the forces of nature and the Universe, I therefore ask Thy Holy presence.
O Thou, Eternal Draconic Force born form the One, by whom Thou manifest yourself, Thou who shines and vibrates through all things, I ask Thee to be assigned a Familiar Dragon who will be my companion and faithful assistant; a brave and wise Draconic Guardian, for the time that will be allotted to me.
Let him come to me, free of choice, and manifest himself in the names of Draconia and the One.
Again, I humbly ask, as a disciple of Draconia and of Cosmic Laws, and by the approval of the Draconic Kings, that a Familiar Dragon be granted unto me, here and now, to serve as a protective guide and assist me in my personal, magickal and spiritual quest.

Trace Active Heptagram in the East, vibrating and making the Sign of the Enterer: **VOVIN-DRACONIS**

Trace Active Heptagram in the South, vibrating and making the Sign of the Enterer: **VOVIN-DRACONIS** Trace Passive Heptagram in the West, vibrating and making the Sign of the Enterer: **VOVIN-DRACONIS** Trace Passive Heptagram in the North, vibrating and making the Sign of the Enterer: **VOVIN-DRACONIS** Seal the light circle and return to the center of the circle facing East.

- *Part Two: The Astral Manifestation*

Take three deep breaths, focus, then right hand on your heart, say:
O Thou, Eternal Draconic Force born form the One, by whom Thou manifest yourself, Thou who shines and vibrates through all things, I ask Thee to be assigned a Familiar Dragon, here and now, in this Draconic Temple.
For the time that will be allotted to me, as a disciple of Draconia and of Cosmic Laws, let a faithful and Familiar Dragon be granted unto me, here and now, to serve as a protective guide and assist me in my personal, magickal and spiritual quest.
Let him come to me, free of choice.
Dragon: manifest, manifest, manifest!

Take a pause in silence then continue:
OL LRING-ILS THEY GAH VOVIN DO TOFGLO DS CHIS DOOAIN BUSD OD MICALZO IAD DRILPA DS I DRILPI OMP.

NIIS: CHRISTEOS FAORGT AFFA.
IMVAMAR LAIAD OD GNAY NANAEEL.
ZAMRAN PUJO-OOANOAN, GOHOL LAIAD DO-
BIAN OD DO-OMP.
VOVIN ZAMRAN PUJO-OOANOAN,
ZAMRAN PUJO-OOANOAN,
ZAMRAN PUJO-OOANOAN!

When the dragon appears, greet him with the Triple
Sign and add:
VOVIN, NIIS ASPT A OD AR A, QUASB OD
BABALON.
VOVIN, GOHO HAS ANANAEL OD FISIS IADNAH.
VOVIN, A NOQOL HOATH OD LONSHI, ODO A
DRACONIA!

• *Part Three: The Instruction and Discharge*

Instruct you new familiar, etc.
Recite the discharge, thus:
Go in peace, Familiar Dragon and assistant magician.
You can return to your Sphere of origin. By my simple
call, whether verbal or mental, come to me, haste, and
listen to receive the instructions I will have to give
you. May we be one in Draconia, Steloi!

Give the Triple Sign.
Perform the Closing Rite.

# THE DRACONIC JOURNEY

T HE draconic Journey, also known as *riding the dragon*,
is an authentic and quite extraordinary ritual. It is
very rewarding for the daraco. The goal is to call
upon a guide or familiar dragon to fly with him to explore
the mysteries and unknown depths of the human soul,
of the Earth and the Universe. As soon as you leave the
ground, this draconic Being will take you to a place where
he needs to, in order to instruct you on various and important matters of your concern or, again, to reveal marvels
and other fantastic things.

Note that it is possible, on some occasions, that the
dragon who will answer your call and you will ride is totally unknown to you. If it happens, know that the Draconic
Force has this power of intervention and has probably de-
cided so for your own good, to present this new winged
guide for his qualities, value, wisdom and judgment. If the
latter agrees to give you his name, you will then be able to
contact him later to benefit again from his knowledge.

You will need to have your grimoire at hand or any
notebook and a pen, so you can transcribe the in details
what happened during your journey, as soon as you re-

turn, that is, at the end of the ritual. As you frequently journey with dragons, it will happen, maybe often, that the information they have shared feels somehow fragmentary or does not necessarily coincide with immediate events in your life. Sometimes what was revealed will be about the past, while at other times, the present or things to come. That's why, by writing down all that is pertaining to your draconic journeys, as you go along, will you be able to check back and see what event will match what you saw on one of your previous flights.

The Rite

This ritual should take place in the evening, preferably on a night of a waxing moon, in your magickal temple or better, in a clearing, a woodland or any other quiet place. It is imperative not to be disturbed.

Start by performing the ritual of the Draconic Cross followed by the ritual of the Hexagram, making sure your magick circle is large enough so that you can lie down at ease without touching the edges. If you are able to do so, then continue with the Opening Rite. Of course, if you are outside, you will be unable to complete the latter unless you have your altar or all your draconic tools at hand. In this case, the draconic Cross and Hexagram rituals should prove sufficient.

Then trace a pentagram inside the circle with your magick wand, dagger, sword or mentally using the index finger of your right hand, so that the upper tip is facing

East. See as you draw, soft burning flames sprout from the ground to form a flaming five-pointed star. Then, place a candle on each point of the pentagram, inside the circle. Light them, starting with the Eastern one and so on clockwise. Finally, light up some dragon's blood incense if you wish and place it in the East, in front of the candle. You are now ready to begin your draconic Journey.

Kneel facing East, in the center of your pentagram. Feel the warmth of the glowing flames all around you. Center yourself in silence, take a few deep breaths, and then focus your attention on dragons, these majestic and wise beings. Try hard establishing a mental contact with them.

When you feel ready, proceed with the call as follows:

Draconis, draconis, draconis!
Dragon companions, fellows in Draconia,
Whatever your names be,
I'm calling you here and now, with me (*your daraco name*)**, the Daraco.**
By my desire for knowledge and perfection,
I ask that one of you take me on a Journey where he deem necessary.
Share with me your Occult Knowledge and great Wisdom,
So I may explore the unknown depths of man, of the Earth and of the Cosmos.
Pure of heart, I ask to fly with one of you.
Draconis, draconis, draconis!

Now lie on your back with your head towards the East. Close your eyes and take a deep breath, waiting for a dragon to come to you and manifest himself at the boundaries of the circle. When you can feel his presence, *mentally get up and leave your physical body.* See it calm, resting peacefully where you lay down as if asleep. Mount and ride the dragon. Feel the strength of his powerful wings pushing the air as the two of you soar into the night sky...

From this point on, don't try controlling your thoughts, let them go where they will take you (or rather where your flight companion will decide). You may end up falling asleep at some point. Don't worry because your subconscious will remember everything for you. Your dragon guide can lead you into subtle, unsuspected realms, fly over unknown lands, mountains, rivers or forest to instruct you on various topics that later will prove of great importance to you. Trust him. Dragons are noble beings. He is here with you, especially to help you in your quest for perfection and magickal development. You will be able to experience vivid emotions, as well as strange and incomprehensible. Be very attentive to your surroundings, and above all, to the wise words of your dragon.

THE RETURN

When your dragon has completed its journey and feels it's time for you to return until you meet again, you'll be brought back in front of your magickal circle, where you left your physical body, inside the pentagram. Get off your mount and enter your physical envelope, leaving the astral world. Open your eyes.

Stand up and face East once more. You will notice that the dragon who accompanied you is still there, calmly waiting for the ritual protocol; that is, the discharge and thanks. Put your right knee on the ground, place your right hand on your heart and thank him for this wonderful flight as follows:

Draconis, draconis, draconis,
Whatever your name is (or say it, if he gave it to you),
I thank you, fellow dragon, for the knowledge you
shared with me.
Until the next Draconic Journey, go back to your
kindred,
And may peace between you and us be eternal, under
the bright rays of High Draconia.
STELOI.

Solemnly give the Triple Sign with your right hand.

Take care to write down in your grimoire all that you can remember of this experience, in images as well as in words, feelings and emotions. Conclude with the Closing Rite (if you performed the Opening Rite).

This completes the Draconic Journey.

THE DRAGON EYE EVOCATION

THERE are certain rites by which the power of dragons can be called and bring into physical manifestation. The Draconic Force, sometimes materialized by the practice of this magickal evocation can even lead directly to the physical appearance of a dragon.

The Dragon Eye Rite will allow you to evoke the Sphere of Draconic Force, straight from its nucleus of power. Once the call is made, it will be up to you to find out what's next, because depending on your degree of mastery in Magick, who knows exactly what can happen?

At dawn or in the evening, choose a quiet place in nature, in a wood, clearing or forest, so you will not be disturbed by anything during the entire evocation.

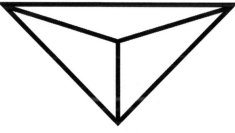

The Dragon's Eye

You will place twelve stones in a circular fashion at equal distances from each other. Now trace a magick circle with your sword or dagger, or mentally by performing the Draconic Cross ritual. Take some iron filings and sprinkle them on the ground, circumambulating clockwise the boundaries of your circle. Finally, with your sword or dagger, trace the symbol of the Dragon's Eye in the center of the circle. This symbol must be large enough for you to stand inside. Please note that you can draw it with flour if you need to refer to a visual guide. Burn some dragon's blood incense. Everything is now ready for this evocation practice.

Take place in the exact center of the Dragon's Eye and visualize that beneath your feet, deep into the Earth, lies a great and radiant sphere of fire. It is overly hot and holds such a strength that you cannot comprehend its full potential; this incredible power source is the Draconic Force.

Keep this image in mind as you raise your sword with both hands, high in the air above your head, with the tip pointing down. Hold the pose and pronounce three times, in a loud and powerful voice, the Great Dragon Evocation:

Cum saxum saxorum
In duersum montum oparum da
In aetibulum
In quinatum Draconis!

At the same time, plunge the blade into the ground (the dragon's body) with force, in a single rapid blow. While doing so, close your eyes and see, as you now sit on the ground, with your legs crossed, that a jet of brilliant and extremely bright red flames explodes from the sphere below and rises at full speed towards the surface of the

Earth. This light pierces all the layers of the Earth in its path until it meets the Eye of the Dragon.

Remain calm and silent, keeping your eyes closed and wait for the arrival of the Draconic Power you have summoned. Remember that the degree of manifestation you might expect will vary between a subtle or ethereal materialization of the Draconic Force up to the physical appearance of a dragon. Remove the sword from the ground to conclude the ritual and return this draconic manifestation.

THE ILLUMINATION OF DRACO

T HERE is a sacred rite among daracos, of such splendor that you cannot imagine it until you put it into practice. It is the Great Ceremony of Light bearing admirably the name of The Illumination of Draco. Obviously, this is one of the most powerful draconic Major Rites.

Its practice will allow you to wear the draconic cloak and wrap yourself in a vestment of Cosmic Light, tinged with the radiating aura of dragons. In other words, you will be able, through this rite, to fill yourself with light, like a shining armor, illuminating everything around you. This cloak of pure energies will be the direct result of the Universal Force of the One, your Supreme Being and the power of the dragons.

The more this Light intensifies inside and outside your physical body, the more its radiation will protect and purify you, consuming all that is discordant, negative or karmic. You'll see all these wrong creations dissolve and leave you forever. The Illumination of Draco will become a protective shield that no thought, feeling or human suggestion will be able to disturb or penetrate. Some very experienced and trained magicians are even able to intensify this luminous aura to such a powerful extent that *even a bullet fired by a pistol would not go through!*

Certainly, during your first tries, it is very possible that you experience difficulties to endure this energy dose for a long time, as its vibration will be highly and extremely charged. Occasionally, when the ritual is performed to perfection, some practitioners may stumble, become dizzy, or even at times, momentarily lose consciousness. Do you realize the full magnitude of this high draconic ritual and how great the power generated can be? Because yes, it is, and so much more...

THE RITE

When the constellation of Draco is perfectly visible in the night sky, winding between the Great and the Little Bear, whether you are outside or in your magickal temple, close your eyes and take three deep breaths. Since this is a fire ritual, some candles can be lit to intensify the light rays. Now, put your right hand on your heart or open your arms in the shape of a cross, palms upwards, and proceed to the call of Light, taking care to visualize the action of your every word:

Great Cosmic Light,
Command, command, command!
Great Cosmic Light,
Manifest, manifest, manifest!
Great Cosmic Light,

Purify, purify, purify!
Great Cosmic Light,
Shine, shine, shine!
Great Cosmic Light,
Liberate, liberate, liberate!

Great Beam of Draconic Light,
Command, command, command!
Great Beam of Draconic Light,
Manifest, manifest, manifest!
Great Beam of Draconic Light,
Intensify, intensify, intensify!
Great Beam of Draconic Light,
Shine, shine, shine!
Great Beam of Draconic Light,
Blaze, blaze, blaze!

I am Daraco, I am Light, I love your Light!
AYAM, I am the Resurrection and Life,
Manifest, manifest, manifest!
AYAM, I am Ascension,
Manifest, manifest, manifest!
Great Cosmic Light descend!
And manifest your Victory now!
Great Beam of Draconic Light, shine!
And show your Victory now!
Great Illumination of the One, great Illumination of
Draco, liberate!
And manifest your Victory now in this sacred Altar
of flesh and blood!

Cosmic Light, Draconic Light, as powerful as thousand of Suns,
Cloak of Light, consume now all that is less than your Purity!
The host of Light Beings and the Dragons' Chain of Wisdom,
Flood my being and body, my soul and spirit, with Pure Light.

AYAM, I am the Daraco, the Flame that cleanses everything,
Clarifies everything, illuminates everything!
Dragons of Power, Heavenly Dragons,
Burst forth your Illumination flames that command,
Shine Your Victory of Pure,
And purify me in Your Fire!
STELOI!

Remain in this exceptional light for as long as you wish Embrace its bliss and feel its action manifesting within you, just as it does outside your body. Conclude by giving the Triple Sign.

THE SUPREME DRACONIC
INVOCATION OF THE HEPTAGRAM

THIS ritual is aptly named. This is the ceremonial technique *par excellence* for invoking the Draconic, Elemental (Sephirotic) and Universal Forces. Admittedly, one of the most complex Major Rites, however, the results obtained are extraordinary. No one could explain you in detail the sensations felt by the practice of the Supreme Draconic Invocation of the Heptagram (SDIH), except to experience it for yourself, tangibly, through its ritual performance.

The purpose of this ritual is to invoke and bring to you, and in your life, the forces described above to be able to bathe in their influences and, of course, consequently, to achieve control and mastery.

KABBALISTIC ATTRIBUTES OF THE HEPTAGRAM

In order to properly interpret the heptagram traced during the SDIH, certain concepts must first be correctly

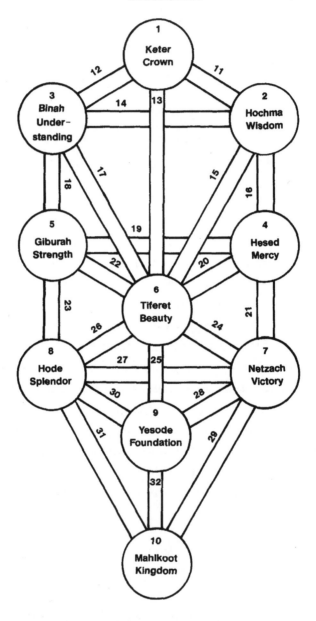

Kabbalistic Tree of Life

understood. The Daraco must know the function of the magickal symbols he uses, if by any means he wants convincing results. The heptagram can be seen from different angles. So, let's start by making the connections that exist with the Kabbalistic Tree of Life. By revealing the correlations between the different interpretive systems, the rest, as you will see, will suddenly become much clearer.

The Tree of Life can be seen as some kind of esoteric diagram containing several truths and showing many analogies, much as one find with other symbols, such as the Yin and the Yang. In fact, it is the foundation of all the science expressed by Kabbalah. If you look at the diagram on the previous page, you will notice that the Kabbalistic Tree of Life consists of ten spheres arranged the form of triangles; three in total. The first triangle is pointing upward while the other two are oriented downwards. Finally, only one sphere remains isolated at the bottom of the Tree. What I describe as spheres are actually named *Sephiroth*, hence the name Sephirotic Tree. Each sphere is called *Sephirah* and they are all connected to each other by 22 paths (equal to the number of cards of the Arcana Major of tarot, as well as the number of letters contained in the Hebrew alphabet), numbered from 11 to 32.

Each Sephira has many associations. Among others, an archangel, an angelic order, a chakra, a divine name, a planet, a creature, a magickal tool, a plant, etc. Moreover, each Sephirah also represents an order of preconceived ideas as well as qualities associated with the symbolic definition of each one, like understanding, wisdom, mercy, strength and beauty, to name a few.

Now, if we connect all the Sephiroth together by drawing a line, from the 1st Sephirah, Kether, to the 10th, Malkoot, we thus obtain the following graphic designated as the Flaming Sword, the same held by the Archangel Michael. The path taken by this sword is the same as the one taken by the Divine to create the world, still according to the Kabbalistic cosmogony.

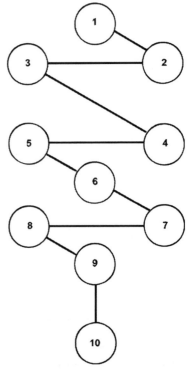

What is important for you to remember is that the three triangles obtained, in addition to the last Sephira at the very bottom, all correspond to one of the *Four Worlds*; another symbolism attributed to the Sephirotic Tree. Thus, the upper triangle (Sephirah 1, 2, 3) is called the *Celestial Triangle* and symbolizes Aholam Atziloot; the World of Archetypes and Emanations. Associated with the Divine, it begins with the highest Sephira, then divides itself in two, demonstrating that Divinity is unity, the One. This representation explains that one of the duties of the daraco is to succeed in abstracting duality in order to come closer to the Divine, recognizing this duality in ways of complementarity and not adversity or opposites. Showing wisdom though understanding.

The second triangle (4, 5, 6) is called the *Morality Triangle* and symbolizes Aholam B'ri-yah; the World of Creations. This triangle is associated to the mental plane. By developing strength and mercy, the daraco will succeed in exhibiting his inner beauty which will help in achieving his goals.

The third triangle (7, 8, 9) is called the *Mundane Triangle* and symbolizes Aholam Yetzirah; the World of Formation. This triangle is associated with the astral plane and is the basis of all the possible results to be obtained and manifested on the material plane. To know how to temper splendor and victory through mercy, is the foundation of success over the physical kingdom represented by the 10th Sephirah Malkoot. This is the lesson to learn.

Malkoot, the last Sephira symbolizes Aholam Ahssiah; the World of Actions. This world represents the action of the Elements, and therefore the physical and material manifestations, the physical plane as we know it.

THE PLANES OF EXISTENCE AND THE HEPTAGRAM

As shown, the Sephiroth are thus arranged to form triangles, each expressing a dimension, or *a world*, according to the Kabbalistic interpretation technique used earlier. By using the pattern obtained by the Flaming Sword and applying it to the heptagram, we then come up with the following (Fig. 1).

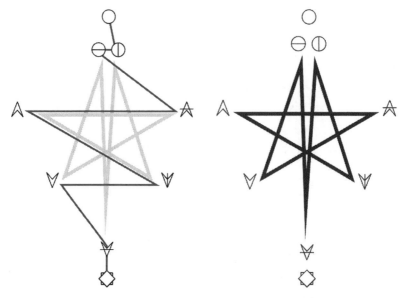

Figure 1
The Flaming Sword traveling
the Heptagram

Figure 2
The Heptagram and the
Planes of Existence

The symbols (Fig. 2) surrounding the heptagram correspond to a Sephirah as well as a different level of consciousness, which is in perfect analogy with the Four Sephirotic Worlds.

We find the heptagram is not only a symbol expressing the qualities of the Tree of Life, but also those related to the planes of existence, namely the Draconic, Elemental, Sephirotic and Universal Forces.

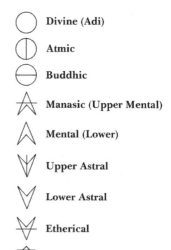

○ Divine (Adi)

⊕ Atmic

⊖ Buddhic

⚛ Manasic (Upper Mental)

△ Mental (Lower)

Ψ Upper Astral

V Lower Astral

⊻ Etherical

◇ Physical

Since this is not a course about Kabbalah, just know the above explanations will prove sufficient to understand and interpret the Kabbalistic attributes of the heptagram put forth in this draconic ritual. As you may see, sometimes if not often, a magickal symbol, simple in appearance, can reveal a very complex and elaborate meaning.

ELEMENTAL ATTRIBUTES OF THE HEPTAGRAM

Finally, there is another method of interpretation of the heptagram, just as there are several ways of reading the Sephirotic Tree. This time, it is the most common way, i.e., the heptagram and the Cosmic Elements. Unlike the pentagram, which has a closed end representing the Element Spirit or Akâsha, this magickal symbol has the same point, but facing downwards. *It is essential* to recognize this point does not mean a continuous extension towards the depths of density, but rather an upward ascent!

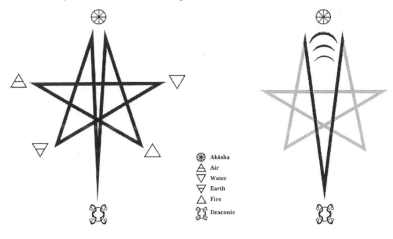

⊛ Akâsha
△ Air
▽ Water
⍦ Earth
△ Fire
⚭ Draconic

This "summit" represents the omnipresent Draconic Force vibrating in everything, manifesting as below so above from the world of matter to the Divine.

The Draconic Force is thus visibly expressed on the physical plane and always pushes upwards, textually speaking, in order to rise to the most subtle and refined planes, until it is melted into the energetic light of the One. That's why this force is so great.

Dear daraco, take all the time necessary to assimilate the matter that has just been reviewed. You will then be able to deduce, with certainty and without fear of being mistaken, that success potential obtained by the practice of the SDIH will be greatly increased, only if you are able to understand the mystery of the heptagram.

THE SUPREME DRACONIC INVOCATION OF THE HEPTAGRAM

Perform the Draconic Cross ritual.
Perform the Draconic Hexagram ritual.
Although the Draconic Cross and the Hexagram ritual are optional, it is still recommended to practice them beforehand.

PART ONE: THE DRACONIC CROSS

Facing the East Watchtower, practice the first part of the Draconic Cross:

Touch your forehead and vibrate: **ZAH**
Point down and vibrate: **ONDOH**
Touch your right shoulder and vibrate: **MIH**
Touch your left shoulder and vibrate: **BUZD**
Then join hands and vibrate: **PAID, STELOI**

PART TWO: THE FORMULATION OF THE HEPTAGRAMS

Head to the boundaries of the circle, in the East, and trace an *Active* Draconic Heptagram, in a continuous line. Visualize it of a very bright and pulsating yellow. Then make the Sign of the Enterer, thrusting both hands into the center of the star, while vibrating:

VOVIN-EXARP (Voh-vee-neh-Etz-har-peh)

Feel the energy penetrating you as you breath in, and then be expelled through your body and hands, into the center of the Heptagram. Take your initial position.

Now trace a bright yellow Invoking Heptagram of Air, over the previous one, while vibrating: **SAIRYS**.

Once again, feel the energy penetrating you and then expelled as you make the Sign of the Enterer, vibrating:

ORO-IBAH-AOZPI (Oh-roh-Eh-bah-Ah-oh-zod-peh)

Finally, over the two Heptagrams, trace the Flaming Sword in pure white light, following the diagram. Vibrate:

OLIMVLDTDCDD
(Oh-leh-meh-veh-leh-deh-teh-deh-cah-deh-deh)

This magickal word of power is composed of the first letter of each word of the following Enochian phrase, which means:

OL LRING-ILS, MICALZO VOVINA, LIALPRT,
DO TOFGLO DS CHIS DOOAIN DRILPA
"I evoke you, Draconic Force, First Flame,
in all things which are the names of the One."

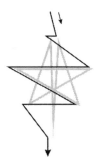

From the center of the Heptagrams, draw a white line while circumambulating to the South. Visualize this line of a very vivid white. The latter will connect all the magickal symbols together.

Facing South, trace the *Active* Draconic Heptagram. Visualize it of a bright pulsating red. Make the Sign of the Enterer, while vibrating:

VOVIN-BITOM (Voh-vee-neh-Bee-toh-meh)

Feel the energy penetrate you as you breath in, and then being expelled through your body and hands, into the center of the Heptagram. Take your initial position.

Trace an Invoking Heptagram of Fire in very bright red, over the previous one, while vibrating: **FAFNYR**.

Once again, feel the energy penetrate you and then being expelled as you make the Sign of the Enterer, vibrating:

OIP-TEAA-PDOKE
(Oh-ee-peh-Teh-ah-ah-Peh-doh-keh)

Finally, over the previous Heptagrams, trace the Flaming Sword while vibrating:

OLIMVLDTDCDD
(Oh-leh-meh-veh-leh-deh-teh-deh-cah-deh-deh)

Point at the center of the Heptagrams and draw a white line while circumambulating to the West.

Facing West, trace a *Passive* Draconic Heptagram. Visualize it of a bright pulsating blue. Then make the Sign of the Enterer, while vibrating:

VOVIN-HCOMA (Voh-vee-neh-Heh-coh-mah)

Feel the energy penetrate you as you breath in, and then being expelled through your body and hands, into the center of the Heptagram. Take your initial position.

Trace an Invoking Heptagram of Water in very bright blue, over the previous one, while vibrating: **NAËLYAN**.

Once again, feel the energy penetrate you and then being expelled as you make the Sign of the Enterer, vibrating:

MPH-ARSL-GAIOL
(Em-peh-heh-Ar-ess-el-Gah-eh-oh-leh)

Finally, trace the Flaming Sword while vibrating:

OLIMVLDTDCDD
(Oh-leh-meh-veh-leh-deh-teh-deh-cah-deh-deh)

Point at the center of the Heptagrams and draw a white line while circumambulating to the North.

Facing North, trace the *Passive* Draconic Heptagram. Visualize it of a bright pulsating green. Then make the Sign of the Enterer, while vibrating:

VOVIN-NANTA (Voh-vee-neh-Nah-en-tah)

Feel the energy penetrate you as you breath in, and then being expelled through your body and hands, into the center of the Heptagram. Take your initial position.

Trace an Invoking Heptagram of Earth in very bright green, over the previous one, while vibrating: **GRAEL**.

Once again, feel the energy penetrate you and then being expelled as you make the Sign of the Enterer, vibrating:

MOR-DIAL-HKTGA
(Moh-ar-Dee-ah-leh-Heh-keh-teh-gah)

Finally, trace the Flaming Sword while vibrating:

OLIMVLDTDCDD
(Oh-leh-meh-veh-leh-deh-teh-deh-cah-deh-deh)

Seal the circle of light as you circumambulate to your starting point in the East. Then return to your initial position in the center of the magickal circle behind your altar. Facing East, take the time to visualize and contemplate all the Heptagrams and Flaming Swords surrounding you and shining with incredible vivacity.

PART THREE: THE EVOCATION OF THE DRACONIC KINGS

Open your arms and say:
Before me stands SAIRYS
Behind me stands NAËLYAN
To my right stands FAFNYR
To my left stands GRAËL
For about me flames the Draconic Pentagram,
And within me shines the Six-rayed Star.

Part Four: The Draconic Cross

Touch your forehead and vibrate: **ZAH**
Point down and vibrate: **ONDOH**
Touch your right shoulder and vibrate: **MIH**
Touch your left shoulder and vibrate: **BUZD**
Then join hands and vibrate: **PAID, STELOI**

From this point, you can perform any kind of occult or draconic work. Or just close your eyes and bathe in this powerful energy. It is strongly recommended to conclude this ritual with the Draconic Cross seeing to banish energies invoked to their respective abodes.

*
**

SUMMARY OF THE SUPREME DRACONIC INVOCATION OF THE HEPTAGRAM (SDIH)

Perform the Draconic Cross ritual.
Perform the Draconic Hexagram ritual.

- *Part One: The Draconic Cross*

  Touch your forehead and vibrate: **ZAH**
  Point down and vibrate: **ONDOH**
  Touch your right shoulder and vibrate: **MIH**
  Touch your left shoulder and vibrate: **BUZD**
  Then join hands and vibrate: **PAID, STELOI**

- *Part Two: The formulation of the Heptagrams*

  Trace Active Draconic Heptagram. Make the Sign of the Enterer, vibrating: **VOVIN-EXARP**
  Trace Invoking Heptagram of Air, vibrating: **SAIRYS**.
  Make the Sign of the Enterer, vibrating: **ORO-IBAH-AOZPI**
  Trace Flaming Sword. Vibrate: **OLIMVLDTDCDD**
  Trace the white line to the South.

  Trace Active Draconic Heptagram. Make the Sign of the Enterer, vibrating: **VOVIN-BITOM**
  Trace Invoking Heptagram of Fire, vibrating: **FAFNYR**.
  Make the Sign of the Enterer, vibrating: **OIP-TEAA-PDOKE**

Trace Flaming Sword. Vibrate: **OLIMVLDTDCDD**
Trace the white line to the West.

Trace Passive Draconic Heptagram. Make the Sign of
the Enterer, vibrating: **VOVIN-HCOMA**
Trace Invoking Heptagram of Water, vibrating:
NAËLYAN.
Make the Sign of the Enterer, vibrating: **MPH-ARSL-GAIOL**
Trace Flaming Sword. Vibrate: **OLIMVLDTDCDD**
Trace the white line to the North.

Trace Passive Draconic Heptagram. Make the Sign of
the Enterer, vibrating: **VOVIN- NANTA**
Trace Invoking Heptagram of Earth, vibrating: **GRAEL**.
Make the Sign of the Enterer, vibrating: **MOR-DIAL-HKTGA**
Trace Flaming Sword. Vibrate: **OLIMVLDTDCDD**
Trace the white line East and complete the circle.

- *Part Three: The Evocation of the Draconic Kings*

Open your arms, forming a cross, and say:
Before me stands SAIRYS
Behind me stands NAËLYAN
To my right stands FAFNYR
To my left stands GRAËL
For about me flames the Draconic Pentagram,
And within me shines the Six-rayed Star.

- *Part Four: The Draconic Cross*

Touch your forehead and vibrate: **ZAH**
Point down and vibrate: **ONDOH**
Touch your right shoulder and vibrate: **MIH**
Touch your left shoulder and vibrate: **BUZD**
Then join hands and vibrate: **PAID, STELOI**

MAY THE LIGHT BE WITH YOU...

IT is our sincere wish that this book has brought you something new and opened your mind to new horizons. But even more, by this knowledge now unveiled, that it became possible for you to see how great and, consequently, powerful High Magick is to serious students wishing to implement the Universal Laws.

Today, you have discovered a new aspect of Magick. However, you should know that Magick is a Unique science, just like the One. The Draconic Teachings of True Dragon Magick are only one aspect of the same versatile and so magnificent source.

Dear friend reader, magician or daraco, if you have been amazed, educated and guided, if you have now found this flame, which

Draconic Heptagram as received by M-A Ricard through meditation

from this moment, will illuminate your steps on the initiatory path of Magick, of Draconia and of spirituality, then
our efforts will not have been in vain. Do good while you
are on this Earth that has been lent to you, while we dragons, on our side, will continue to watch over you. May the
sparkling Light of Draconia and the One shine on you
permanently...

~ PNFYR & M-A R

RECOMMENDED READINGS

F OR those who wish to perfect their Art and training towards the highest spheres of personal, magickal and spiritual development, I strongly recommend the following titles. Not only will you find new and interesting concepts, even essential ones, but you will be able to perfect the teachings of this book.

Franz Bardon, *Initiation into Hermetics*
Franz Bardon, *The Practice of Magical Evocation*
Franz Bardon, *The Key to the True Kabbalah*
Alice A. Bailey, *A Treatise on White Magic*
Papus, *Elementary Treatise on Practical Magic*
Donald Michael Kraig, *Modern Magick, Eleven Lessons in the High Magickal Arts*
Gerald Schueller, *Enochian Magick*
Omraam Mikhael Aïvanhov, *The Book of Divine Magic*
A. Farnese, *Franchezzo, A Wandered in the Spirit Lands*
A. & D. Meurois-Givaudan, *Reports of an Astral Traveler*

APPENDIX

TABLE OF PENTAGRAMS, HEXAGRAMS, HEPTAGRAMS AND OTHER SYMBOLS

Draconic Cross
Banishing Pentagram of the Earth

Draconic Hexagram Ritual
Unicursal Hexagram

Draconic Opening Ritual
Invoking Pentagrams

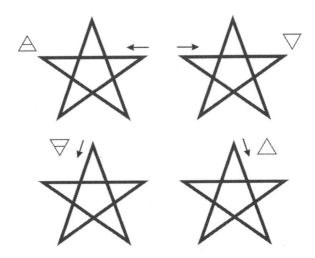

Major Rite of the Familiar Dragon

Active Draconic Heptagram   Passive Draconic Heptagram

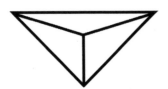

Dragon Eye Evocation
Dragon's Eye

The Supreme Draconic Invocation of the Heptagram

Symbols and Planes of Existence

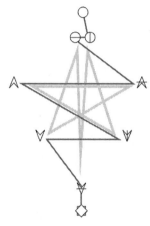

Flaming Sword traveling
the Heptagram

The Heptagram and the
Planes of Existence

Active Draconic
Heptagram

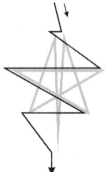

Flaming Sword

Passive Draconic
Heptagram

Invoking   Invoking   Invoking   Invoking
Heptagram   Heptagram   Heptagram   Heptagram
of Air   of Fire   of Water   of Earth

TABLE OF CONTENTS

CAPUT DRACONIS
Head of the Dragon

CORPUS DRACONIS
Body of the Dragon

CODA DRACONIS
Tail of the Dragon

Made in the USA
Middletown, DE
14 February 2025

71366207R00138